INVASION OF PRIVACY

INVASION OF PRIVACY

William Zelermyer

SYRACUSE UNIVERSITY PRESS

LIBRARY OF CONGRESS CATALOG CARD NUMBER: 59-15386

© 1959 by SYRACUSE UNIVERSITY PRESS

MANUFACTURED IN THE UNITED STATES OF AMERICA

Preface

On October 25, 1758, a discourse on the study of law, written by Sir William Blackstone, was read in the public schools of England. Its purpose was to impress upon the youth of that day the conviction that none could consider himself well educated without a competent knowledge of the law "which is to be the guardian of his natural rights, and the rule of his civil conduct."

Today, in America, most of what is learned in the law is acquired within the confines of law schools. The public at large is given a glimpse of the law through *Perry Mason, The Lone Ranger, Dragnet, Code 3,* and various other forms of television entertainment. While these dramatizations may be successful so far as their particular aims are concerned, they provide little opportunity for acquiring a "competent knowledge" of the law. What is needed is a more informative level of communication between the lawyer and the layman.

The field of law is so immense that any attempt to impart a knowledge of its entire substance would be futile. Moreover, a cursory survey of its fabric would produce little enlightenment and could result in grave misconceptions. How, then, can Blackstone's hope be fulfilled?

It would be a gross exaggeration to say that this volume provides the answer, but this work is intended as an attempt to make a bold advance in that direction. Realizing the impossibility of giving beneficial coverage to a wide variety of areas in one volume, it seems that a proper beginning can be made by an extensive treatment of a single but important segment of the law. What better subject could be chosen for the purpose than that which lies at the heart of all human rights—privacy? This is the term by which we indicate our respect for the individual. This is the term which enables individuals to call some things their own. Privacy encompasses all matters considered private as distinguished from public. Public affairs are concerned with collective endeavors, while private affairs are concerned with individual interests and aspirations. However, even the collective endeavors of the public are aimed at the promotion and preservation of individual well-being and advancement. Freedom has no meaning except as it is associated with the life and liberty of individuals. Hence, the concept of privacy should occupy a primary position in the minds of all human beings.

It is not the object here to deal with privacy in all of its aspects, but rather to concentrate on that aspect with which the courts have most frequently been directly confronted. While touching upon other aspects in the first and last chapters, for the purpose of indicating the involvement of privacy in current public issues, the bulk of this work presents the development of the right of privacy as a concept in the realm of civil wrongs called torts.

The study of any portion of the law involves a close examination of the cases reported under a particular heading. Those cases which fall under the heading of privacy are peculiarly well suited to the purpose of this undertaking, for the factual situations they present are simple to comprehend and fascinating to contemplate. They are replete with human interest. At the same time, the issues they raise are thought-provoking, and the decisions given provide an adequate insight into legal reasoning.

The presentation of many cases should not be taken as the result of a design to fill space. A careful examination will reveal that seemingly similar cases have distinguishing features, or that cases having similar factual situations are reviewed for the purpose of showing various treatments by different courts. It should also be pointed out that the many quotations found herein have been included for the purpose of bringing the reader into direct contact with judicial expression and reasoning. The work thus represents a page torn from legal literature and presented with explanations and provocative comments. The purpose pursued is to promote enlightenment and to stimulate an active interest in the laws by which we are governed.

Considering the purpose of this work, as well as the nature of its subject-matter, it seems appropriate to forego the scholarly practice of including complete citations of the cases used. Those who feel so inclined may easily find the cases on privacy in the law reports. For the sake of the lay reader, formality has been avoided.

Heartfelt thanks are extended to Ralph E. Kharas, Dean of the College of Law, Syracuse University, in gratitude for his constructive criticism and helpful suggestions, which guided the revision and improvement of the original manuscript. I am especially grateful to my wife, Herma H. Zelermyer, who assumed the role of layman-critic and helped to keep the manuscript within the bounds of common comprehension.

WILLIAM ZELERMYER
Professor of Business Law, Syracuse University
Member of the New York Bar

Contents

Grand View

On the morning of Tuesday, June 18, 1957, every reader of the *New York Times* found his eyes fixed upon the following headline: "HIGH COURT FREES WATKINS, CURBS CONGRESS' INVASION OF PRIVACY." Because of the great lapse of time that usually separates an event and the final determination of its legal significance, perhaps only a few of those who read the headline could automatically recollect the nature of the case or immediately appreciate the impact of its decision. A little reflection, however, revealed that this was a Supreme Court decision regarding the rights of individuals subjected to the unremitting probing of Congressional investigations.

The McCarthy Committee and the Kefauver Committee, aided by television, had given notoriety to the character and operational effects of congressional investigations.

The Fifth Amendment had become a household term meaning the veil behind which to hide criminal and Communist activities. So far as the public was concerned Congress, through committees and subcommittees, was bent on cleaning up intolerable messes. Little thought was given to propriety and legality. Fear hovered above the populace and helped becloud the basic issues as they arose in the struggle between the individual and the champions of the people. Some champions operated with such enthusiasm and determination that, taking a grand view of their missions, they caused the committee room to assume the appearance of a Star Chamber. To the casual onlooker, it appeared as though our judicial system had changed, and that congressional subcommittees had replaced the criminal courts. Some individuals faced their interrogators with boldness, insisting upon their rights and challenging the authority of those who sought to compel revelations. The interrogators answered with charges of contempt and relied upon the courts to uphold their views and to inflict the proper punishment.

The Watkins case arose out of an investigation by a subcommittee of the Un-American Activities Committee of the House of Representatives. This committee was established by a House resolution passed in 1938 and later became a standing committee of that legislative body.

Its first chairman was Congressman Martin Dies. Its authority was defined by the resolution as follows:

> The Committee on Un-American Activities, as a whole or by subcommittee, is authorized to make from time to time investigations of (I) the extent, character, and objects of un-American propaganda activities in the United States, (II) the diffusion within the United States of subversive and un-American propaganda that is instigated from foreign countries or of a domestic origin and attacks the principle of the form of government as guaranteed by our Constitution, and (III) all other questions in relation thereto that would aid Congress in any necessary legislation.

John Thomas Watkins appeared before a subcommittee of the Un-American Activities Committee on April 29, 1954, in response to a subpoena. He had been a union official since 1942, serving the Farm Equipment Workers until 1953 when he joined the United Automobile Workers. His schooling had ended with the eighth grade in Mount Sterling, Iowa, and he had worked at various jobs until 1935, when he became an employee of the International Harvester Company. He had been given a leave of absence by the company in 1942 in order to enable him to assume the responsibilities of a union official. The leave had been in effect until 1953, when his status as an employee was terminated. Why had he been summoned for questioning? Because two witnesses at previous hearings had testified that Watkins had recruited them into the Communist party. Both had hastened to add that they were no longer members of the party. Upon being confronted with these accusations Watkins, with unreproachable demeanor, gave this candid reply:

> I am not now nor have I ever been a card-carrying member of the Communist party. Rumsey was wrong when he said I had recruited him into the party, that I had received his dues, that I paid dues to him, and that I had used the alias Sam Brown.
>
> Spencer was wrong when he termed any meetings which I attended as closed Communist party meetings.
>
> I would like to make it clear that for a period of time from approximately 1942 to 1947 I cooperated with the Community party and participated in Communist activities to such a degree that some persons may honestly believe that I was a member of the party.
>
> I have made contributions upon occasions to Communist causes. I have signed petitions for Communist causes. I attended caucuses at an F.E. convention at which Communist party officials were present.
>
> Since I freely cooperated with the Communist party I have no motive for making the distinction between cooperation and membership except the simple fact that it is the truth. I never carried a Communist party card.

I never accepted discipline and indeed on several occasions I opposed their position.

In a special convention held in the summer of 1947 I led the fight for compliance with the Taft-Hartley Act by the FE-CIO International Union. This fight became so bitter that it ended any possibility of future cooperation.

The subcommittee seemed pleased in having been accorded so frank a reply, and it seemed to them that Watkins would be equally frank in answering one further query. Rumsey, one of Watkins' accusers, had furnished the committee with a list of thirty-three persons known to him as members of the Communist party. Here was a frank and willing witness—why not ask him about the thirty-three alleged Communists? And so the subcommittee proposed that Watkins tell them what he knew about those persons. But Watkins balked and refused to be of further accommodation, explaining his position as follows:

> I am not going to plead the Fifth Amendment, but I refuse to answer certain questions that I believe are outside the proper scope of your committee's activities. I will answer any question which this committee puts to me about myself. I will also answer questions about those persons whom I knew to be members of the Communist party and whom I believe still are. I will not, however, answer any questions with respect to others with whom I associated in the past. I do not believe that any law in this country requires me to testify about persons who may in the past have been Communist party members or otherwise engaged in Communist party activity but who to my best knowledge and belief have long since removed themselves from the Communist movement.
>
> I do not believe that such questions are relevant to the work of this committee nor do I believe that this committee has the right to undertake the public exposure of persons because of their past activities. I may be wrong, and the committee may have this power, but until and unless a court of law so holds and directs me to answer, I must firmly refuse to discuss the political activities of my past associates.

Thus did Watkins challenge the subcommittee to justify the line of questioning it had adopted, and the subcommittee responded by taking steps to have Watkins prosecuted for contempt of Congress. A Federal District Court found him guilty, and the Circuit Court of Appeals affirmed the conviction. But on June 17, 1957, the Supreme Court, by a six-to-one vote, upset the Congressional applecart. In rendering his opinion, Chief Justice Warren gave a profound and pervasive analysis of the investigatory powers of Congress.

The investigative power of Congress is not unlimited. It must be related to legislation, except where the purpose is to expose corruption, inefficiency or waste within departments of the Federal Government. Investigations conducted for the purpose of exposing the private affairs of individuals are without justification. The Chief Justice made his point in this way:

> But broad as is this power of inquiry, it is not unlimited. There is no general authority to expose the private affairs of individuals without justification in terms of the functions of the Congress. This was freely conceded by the Solicitor General in his argument of this case. Nor is the Congress a law enforcement or trial agency. These are functions of the Executive and Judicial departments of Government. No inquiry is an end in itself; it must be related to and in furtherance of a legitimate task of the Congress. Investigations conducted for the personal aggrandizement of the investigators or to "punish" those investigated are indefensible.

The Chief Justice went on to point out that a new type of Congressional inquiry arose following World War II, an inquiry concerned with subversive activities and involving itself with intrusions into the private lives of individuals. The problem of accommodating the interests of Governmnt with the rights of citizens became prominent. What of the Bill of Rights, that sacred bulwark constructed to protect the individual against encroachments by his government? The Fifth Amendment was recognized as a protector against the force that would compel self-incrimination. But how could one repel the invasion of his privacy? Does not one have the right to think as he pleases, go where his footsteps take him, associate as his pleasure dictates? Watkins called upon the First Amendment as his protector:

> Congress shall make no law respecting an establishment of religion, or prohibiting the free exercise thereof; or abridging the freedom of speech, or of the press; or the right of the people peaceably to assemble, and to petition the government for a redress of grievances.

One might retort that the First Amendment prohibited certain laws but not inquiries. The Chief Justice took a broad view:

> Clearly, an investigation is subject to the command that the Congress shall make no law abridging freedom of speech or press or assembly. While it is true that there is no statute to be reviewed, and that an investigation is not a law, nevertheless an investigation is part of lawmaking. It is justified solely as an adjunct to the legislative process. The first amendment may be invoked against infringement of the protected freedoms by law or by lawmaking.
>
> Abuses of the investigative process may imperceptibly lead to abridgement of protected freedoms. The mere summoning of a witness and compelling him to testify, against his will, about his beliefs, expressions, or associations is a measure of Governmental interference. And when those forced revelations concern matters that are unorthodox, unpopular, or

even hateful to the general public, the reaction in the life of the witnesses may be disastrous. This effect is even more harsh when it is past beliefs, expressions or associations that are disclosed and judged by current standards rather than those contemporary with the matters exposed. Nor does the witness alone suffer the consequences. Those who are identified by witnesses and thereby placed in the same glare of publicity are equally subject to public stigma, scorn and obloquy. Beyond that, there is the more subtle and immeasurable effect upon those who tend to adhere to the most orthodox and uncontroversial views and associations in order to avoid a similar fate at some future time. That this impact is partly the result of non-Governmental activity by private persons cannot relieve the investigators of their responsibility for initiating the reaction.

We must be careful to note that the Court did not say that all intrusions upon privacy are barred by the Constitution. Congress does have power to make investigations, and these investigations may lead to exposure of private affairs. Such exposure, however, must have justification to support it, and the required justification may be found only where the investigation is conducted as an adjunct to legislation. There must be a legislative purpose served by the inquiry—a purpose which must be explicit and cannot be assumed. As the Chief Justice states:

> We cannot simply assume, however, that every Congressional investigation is justified by a public need that overbalances any private rights affected. To do so would be to abdicate the responsibility placed by the Constitution upon the judiciary to insure that the Congress does not unjustifiably encroach upon an individual's right to privacy nor abridge his liberty of speech, press, religion or assembly.

Watkins contended that there was no public purpose served by his interrogation, and that the only purpose in the minds of his interrogators was to expose him and others to the wrath of public opinion because of their past beliefs, expressions and associations. He even had evidence to show that some Congressmen were of the belief that such exposures constituted at least a portion of their duties.

What specifically was the purpose that might be said to have justified the inquiry to which Watkins had been subpoenaed? The first clue could be found in the resolution that created the Un-American Activities Committee (quoted above). To this the Chief Justice reacted as follows:

> It would be difficult to imagine a less explicit authorizing resolution. Who can define the meaning of "un-American"? What is the single, solitary "principle of the form of government as guaranteed by our Constitution"? There is no need to dwell upon the language, however. At one time, perhaps, the resolution might have been read narrowly to confine

the Committee to the subject of propaganda. The events that have transpired in the fifteen years before the interrogation of petitioner makes
such a construction impossible at this date.

The members of the committee have clearly demonstrated that they did
not feel themselves restricted in any way to propaganda in the narrow
sense of the word. Unquestionably the committee conceived of its task in
the grand view of its name. Un-American activities were its target, no matter how or where manifested . . .

The resolution, therefore, was found by the Court to be lacking as
an indication of the specific purpose aimed to be served by the inquiry.
Yet, in order for the conviction to stand, the question of purpose would
have to be answered, for the criminal statute under which Watkins
was being prosecuted defined as a misdemeanor the refusal "to answer
any question pertinent to the question under inquiry." What was the
question under inquiry? Surely a witness who has been summoned
to testify is entitled to be made aware of the question under inquiry
if he is to have the opportunity of guarding his right to withhold irrelevant testimony. Entrapment by vagueness can certainly find no
place in the philosophy of due process of law.

The Government contended that the subject under inquiry was
Communist infiltration into labor, since the chairman of the subcommittee, during the course of his opening remarks, had referred to a
pending bill which would penalize unions controlled by past or present members of "Communist-action" organizations, a term defined in
the Internal Security Act of 1950. But the published transcript of the
hearings bore the title "Investigation of Communist Activities in the
Chicago Area." Besides, six of the nine witnesses who appeared before
the committee had nothing to do with labor. Also, seven of the persons about whom Watkins was questioned had no connection whatsoever with labor.

The final bit of evidence bearing on the "question under inquiry"
came from the statement made by the chairman of the subcommittee
when Watkins had refused to answer on the ground that the question
put to him was not pertinent. The chairman stated that the subject
of the investigation was "subversion and subversive propaganda."
"This," observed the Court, "is a subject at least as broad and indefinite
as the authorizing resolution of the committee, if not more so." The
Court further observed:

The statement of the committee chairman in this case, in response to petitioner's protest, was woefully inadequate to convey sufficient information as to the pertinency of the questions to the subject under inquiry. Petitioner was thus not accorded a fair opportunity to determine whether

he was within his rights in refusing to answer, and his conviction is necessarily invalid under the due process clause of the Fifth Amendment.

Justice Clark, the lone dissenter, began his criticism of the majority opinion on the following note:

As I see it the chief fault in the majority opinion is its mischievous curbing of the informing function of the Congress . . .

What followed was a point by point expression of disagreement with the reasoning of the majority. According to Justice Clark, the subject under inquiry was sufficiently explicit and there was no doubt that Watkins was fully informed regarding the subject matter of the inquiry.

There will be those who will agree with the majority and those who will agree with the minority, but the question remains whether ruthless exposure of the past activities of private individuals is necessary in furtherance of the legislative process. Justice Clark thought:

If the parties about whom Watkins was interrogated were Communists and collaborated with him, as a prior witness indicated, an entirely new area of investigation might have been opened up. Watkins' silence prevented the committee from learning this information which could have been vital to its future investigation.

Let us remember that Watkins refused to answer only those questions as related to the past activities of his present or past associates. Watkins could not see the pertinency of such information to any legitimate Congressional inquiry. He had been summoned because others had named him and because he might be instrumental in the exposure of others, who, in turn, would be expected to enlarge the sphere of revelation. Have we not known that thousands upon thousands of our people have in the past embraced and later deserted the ideology of communism? Must interminable effort and precious recourses be wastefully expended to find that they have established themselves in all categories of human endeavor? Are we so naive in this advanced scientific age that we cannot conjecture techniques of infiltration? Surely a committee that has been in operation since 1938 cannot still be looking for information that will lead to suitable combative legislation. That legislation has resulted from recommendations of the committee during the intervening years is no proof that a legislative purpose prompted and controlled each investigation and hearing. It is difficult to dispel the personal conviction that, while the creation of the Un-American Activities Committee in 1938 may have been accompanied by a legislative purpose, its efforts as a permanent committee have been directed toward the elimination of communism as a threat to domestic security by exposure rather than by the enactment of new legislation or the enforcement of current enactments.

What did Justice Clark mean by the "informing function" of Congress? Did he mean the function of informing the public, or the function of becoming informed?

The conclusion seems inescapable that, as put by Chief Justice Warren, the Un-American Activities Committee took a grand view of its functions. If government is to operate according to the mandate of the people, each department must exercise restraint in operating within its designated scope, and the Bill of Rights must be scrupulously observed. It is paradoxical to deny the very rights we have been striving to preserve.

The Watkins case represents the struggle between the interests of the community and the rights of the individual. As indicated by the *New York Times* headline, the central theme is invasion of privacy. The same theme has been found at the core of many civil cases, in a great number of which individual rights have been weighed against the public interest. We shall, in later chapters, discuss such cases as are concerned with the right of privacy. It seems appropriate, however, that we should first take a broad look at the law in operation, in order that our notions of the whole may afford a better appreciation of the portion under consideration.

2

Law
in Operation

To the person who has had no train-
ing in the law, or who has had no
conspicuous relationship with it,
the field of law seems enshrouded
in mystery and obscurity. The mere mention of the subject makes him
feel uneasy. Instead of justice, injustice comes to mind. Almost immediately, he recalls a situation in which right failed to triumph. He
thinks of trickery, showmanship, loopholes, a bored-looking judge, and
a jack rabbit crying "Objection!" His notions of the law come from
television and motion picture dramas concerned mainly with crime,
from novels and magazine stories dealing with the same, or from some
brief personal encounter brought about by an automobile accident or
a death in the family. To him, a lawyer is a person who gets you out
of a jam, who procures a windfall settlement or verdict, who wins the
case regardless of the merits, and who takes for himself a dispropor-
tionate share of the spoils.

Law is not the private property of judges, lawyers, and law pro-
fessors. It is the lifeblood of society. It penetrates the innermost depths
of human relationships and activity. It is omnipresent and eternal,
commanding and demanding, sanctioning and prohibiting, affording
protection and providing vigilance. From birth until death, and even
thereafter, the affairs of man are scrutinized in the light of their legal
significance. The weak are overcome by the strong, the artless by the
artful, the tactless by the tactful, and the ignorant by the informed.
Considering the complexities of current living, some knowledge of
the law is essential to the avoidance of pitfalls and to the realization
of advantages prescribed by law. One cannot rest assured by the
thought that a lawyer will be available when the occasion arises. There
is need for recognizing some occasions, as there is also need for avoiding others. Enlightenment breeds respect and confidence, as well as a
critical and resourceful eye. It is always comforting to understand what
is going on, to know the prospects and alternatives, and, in some cases,
to be able to direct attention toward matters that may have been overlooked.

To the initiate, a taste of legal fare whets the appetite. Though be-

wildered, he soon experiences a sensation of fascination. Though finding it difficult to overcome long-cherished misconceptions, he begins to
see things fitting into place. Prejudice gives way to reason, as darkness
is dispelled by the coming of dawn. But as the novice wends his way
along unfamiliar paths and finds himself in the middle of a forest, only
a sense of direction, added to his confidence, will preserve his com-
posure. He must know the nature of law, its basic tenets, and its mode
of operation. He must see himself as a part of its functioning and
growth. He must have a conception of its structure and texture.

The paths of the law are not straight and narrow. Neither do they
all lead to the same destination, nor do they emanate from all possible
points of embarkation. One who travels along these routes will find
occasional disgressions and diversions, as well as spiral-like courses such
as are common in roads that facilitate ascension to the summit of a
mountain. Some paths are joined by the insertion of bridges, while
others are broken by the erection of dams. Regardless of size, shape,
or direction, the paths of the law form a unified network, with no beginning and no ending. These paths are trodden by human beings,
whose tendency is to follow them. Time or tide, fact or fancy, excuse
or exigency, constraint or construction, may cause pathways to deviate
from their original locations, but the basic pattern of the law maintains
its enduring form.

The legal network is constantly alive. At every moment there is an
infinite variety of situations having legal significance. A child is born
of wedlock, another is born out of wedlock, while a third is being
adopted. A man dies of natural causes, another by suicide, another by
accident brought about by his own neglect, another by accident caused
by the neglect of a second person, another by a combination of his own
neglect and that of a second person, another by the intention or reck-
lessness of a second person, and still another by execution. Men are
forming corporations, partnerships, single proprietorships; signing
deeds, leases, mortgages, bonds, notes, checks, drafts; manufacturing
goods, selling goods, buying goods; lending money, borrowing money;
rendering services, receiving services; making wills, creating trusts; selling businesses, buying businesses; employing persons, being employed,
discharging persons, being discharged; entering marriages, procuring
divorces, separations and annulments; engaging in illicit relationships;
driving carelessly, parking illegally; peeping, eavesdropping; libeling
and slandering; inventing, discovering, procuring patents, infringing
patents; designing trade-marks, infringing trade-marks; copyrighting
and infringing copyrights; engaging in lawful competition and com-

peting unfairly; negotiating and contracting; performing contracts and breaching contracts; wagering and conspiring; defrauding and extorting; admitting and denying; forging and altering documents; finding, losing, and abandoning property; burglarizing and burning; stealing property, assaulting and beating persons, blackmailing; pledging and repudiating; influencing, being influenced; paying and collecting; etc., etc., etc. Legislatures are debating proposals for enactment, repeal, or amendment, while investigating the possibilities and proprieties of strengthening the fabric of legislation. Executives are carrying on the functions of administration, including the maintenance and spread of good will, the management of the business aspects of government, the effectuation of legislation, and the provision of leadership in the progressive advancement of their respective communities. While police cars, ambulances, and fire engines are sirening their way to points of emergency, courts of justice are holding sessions on various levels.

Let us enter a courtroom and take seats in the section reserved for spectators. In this particular courtroom we see a judge, a jury, and two attorneys seated at separate tables with their respective clients. These are the principals in the drama to be unfolded. The casual observer impatiently awaits the commencement of proceedings, unaware of the background that has preceded the present scene, and unfamiliar with the rules that govern the performance about to begin. This is to be no mere sporting event whose background and rules are known among the overwhelming majority of its spectators, nor the presentation of a stage production born of poetic license. The prelude to our courtroom drama takes us back to the beginning of human life in society.

It is difficult, if not impossible, to conceive of any society without law. In forming conceptions as to the operation of law in ages past, we inevitably think of clans and tribes, with chieftains ruling the roost. Life was comparatively simple, but order had to be kept internally, ceremonials had to be observed, and protection against external dangers had to be provided and maintained. There was no notion of individual rights: whatever injury was inflicted was considered an injury to the community; and whatever possessions were acquired were considered the property of the community. Vengeance was the usual redress for wrongs. Regardless of its crudeness, a legal system was in operation. Decisions were being made through the use of the same basic formula as we still use today, the application of rules and principles to factual situations.

When man discovered the value of land, original possession and conquest placed large territories at the disposal of rulers. Upon the allotment of portions to heroes in battle, private interests began. The masses lived in virtual enslavement, but as they began to evaluate the fruits of their labors they rebelled and fought for freedom. As land became more widely distributed and put to productive use, as resources were discovered, as fabrication became an art, as trades developed and trading ensued, the activities of man began to assume an individualistic as well as a communal look. He had land of his own, and possessions of his own; he could deal on his own with others, but always subject to the rules of the community.

Today there is a recognition of individual as well as of communal rights. There is likewise a recognition of individual as well as communal duties. Rights and duties are correlative. Where one person has a right, another person has a duty with respect to that right. Thus, if A has a right to receive $100 from B, B has a duty to pay A $100. But how do we know that A has this right? We know that a person has a right when the law recognizes his power to control the actions of another to the extent of his asserted claim. If A brings an action against B and wins, we know that A has a right against B, and that B has an obligation to act in compliance with that right.

What is the law that recognizes the power of one to control the actions of another? It is the sum total of those rules of human conduct that are given effect by the governing body of a political community.

How do we know what these rules are? We find them mainly in court decisions and in statute books. Whatever rules are given effect and are not found in the statute books constitute the common law, while those that are found in the statute books constitute the statutory law.

What law governs the decision of a court in a particular case? If the applicable rule is found in the statute books, statutory law governs. If the applicable rule is not found in the statute books, common law is used.

While it is fairly simple to appreciate the fact that statutory law results from the enactments of legislatures, whence springs the common law? Custom and usage are its forerunners. When these attributes become firmly entrenched in the understandings and expectations of a community, they are perforce recognized as law. On what other basis, unless it be arbitrary, could the first case of its kind have ever been decided? And now that it has been decided, shall it not be regarded in the making of future decisions in similar cases? We have come to regard previous decisions as precedents.

Do precedents have binding effects? They are binding to the extent that the present court does not feel that the previous decision was arrived at through error, or that present conditions compel a different view.

But what is written law? And what is unwritten law? These are merely terms sometimes used in referring to statutory law and common law respectively. A legislature labors over the exact words to be used for the expression of its will and writes them down for inclusion in the statute books. There was a time when the decisions of courts were not preserved in permanent form, and the impressions of these decisions were conveyed by word of mouth as dictated by memory. Since today the words used in court decisions are found in printed law reports, it seems that the term, unwritten law, has lost its meaning. Nevertheless, since no exact words are required to be used in the recital of a common law rule, and since courts have some measure of discretion in the observation of precedents, there is still reason for referring to the common law as unwritten law.

And do we not often refer to moral law? What is a moral right as distinguished from a legal right? And what is a moral duty as distinguished from a legal duty? The law sets boundaries to legal recognition. It will not delve into the consciences of individuals. Religious teachings lead men to be charitable, but the law provides no compulsion in this direction. One may reward another for a kindness, but the law does not prescribe such reward. What society considers that a man ought to do is his moral duty. What society considers that a man must do is his legal duty. What one ought to get from another is his moral right. What one must give to another is the latter's legal right.

Legal rights fall into two broad classifications, personal and property. Those which the individual alone may enjoy, and for whose invasion no other individual may seek redress, are termed personal rights. Those which the individual may contract away, give away, leave by will, or leave to descend to heirs without a will, are termed property rights. The Declaration of Independence says that all men "are endowed, by their Creator, with certain unalienable rights, that among these are life, liberty, and the pursuit of happiness." Thus, such rights as are therein enumerated are considered personal rights. The United States Constitution, in the Fifth and Fourteenth Amendments, says that no person shall be deprived of "life, liberty, or property, without due process of law." The substitution of "property" in place of "pursuit of happiness" can only mean that the framers of the Amendments felt that the pursuit of happiness was already implicit in the terms, "life"

and "liberty," and that the term, "property," should be added to insure the recognition of property rights among the natural individual
rights of man.

Now, what are natural rights? These are rights that are considered
inherent in man by his very existence. While other rights may be acquired by contract, by gift, by will, or by governmental enactment, natural rights reside in each person from birth until death.

But how can property be considered a natural right? Of course,
property rights are acquired and disposed of through contract, or otherwise, and in that sense are not considered natural rights. However,
when spoken in the same breath with "life" and "liberty," "property"
means the right to acquire and to experience unmolested enjoyment
of property rights. It means that we consider private ownership as
natural a phenomenon of man as the will to live and the will to be
free. Hence, the right to acquire and to enjoy property is a natural
right.

What difference does it make that there are personal rights and
property rights, natural rights and contractual rights? Needless to
say, the body of law is immense, and no individual, in a lifetime, can
explore and comprehend all of its innumerable details. To facilitate
its study and its administration, classifications are necessary, and the
mere mention of a legal term directs attention to that portion of the
law with which a matter may be involved. Moreover, the establishment
of certain terms of reference gives rise to the formulation of principles
which guide the making of decisions in the absence of clear-cut precedents. Thus, in civil actions, tort and contract are comprehensive terms,
while in public prosecutions the basic term is crime.

Naturally, actions in contract grow out of agreements between persons, but what is a tort? A tort is an interference with a natural right
of another. It entitles the injured party to bring an action for damages against the wrongdoer, or to seek whatever other remedy the law
allows with respect to the particular situation. If the public feels that
it, as well as the individual, has been injured, the wrongdoer will be
prosecuted for the commission of a crime.

How does a person bring action against another? Let us say, first
of all, that, although the law does not compel it, the retention of an
attorney is most highly recommended. Even an attorney is considered
foolish when he undertakes to conduct his own action. Assuming that
all possible attempts to secure a peaceful settlement have failed, that
the resort to an action at law has been decided upon, and that a court
having jurisdiction with respect to the particular matter has been se-

lected, the action is begun by the service of a summons upon the adversary.

A summons is a document, issued under the authority of a court, by which a person is apprised of the fact that an action against him has been commenced. It designates the court, names the person bringing the action as plaintiff and his adversary as defendant, calls upon the defendant to answer the complaint within a specified time, and advises the defendant that, unless he answers within that time, judgment will be entered against him by default. The complaint is either attached to the summons, or may be procured from the plaintiff, or his attorney, upon request.

A complaint is a document in which the plaintiff sets forth his cause of action and demands the judgment to which he deems himself entitled. The action is set forth by a listing of allegations, i.e., statements of what the plaintiff contends are the facts. A cause of action is a factual situation which the law recognizes as involving rights that have been interfered with or disregarded. Thus, in his complaint, the plaintiff hurls his challenge to the defendant. The defendant must answer it or surrender.

An answer is a document in which the defendant sets forth his defenses. There are various defenses available, and the defendant may use as many as he feels will be effective to counteract the claims asserted in the complaint. For the purpose of conveying some understanding of legal procedure without getting too technical, we shall deal with only two types of defenses—the general denial and the demurrer.

By using a general denial, the defendant denies the truth of each and every allegation contained in the complaint. If he combines with this no other defense, he is, in effect, admitting that the plaintiff should win if he is successful in proving the truth of his allegations. Thus, such a defense raises a factual issue, the truth or falsity of the allegations, and the proceedings in the courtroom will then be centered around the determination of that issue.

By using a demurrer, the defendant is saying in effect that, even if he were to admit the truth of the allegations, the plaintiff has failed, in his complaint, to state a cause of action. Thus, such a defense raises a legal issue, the existence or nonexistence of a rule of law which, when applied to the facts alleged by the plaintiff, substantiates the plaintiff's claim of right. The proceedings in the courtroom will then be centered about the determination of that issue.

The outcome of a case, therefore, depends upon the determination of the issues raised by the parties through the exchange of documents. The typical portrayal of a courtroom scene presents a proceeding concerned with the trial of factual issues. Proceedings concerned with the trial of legal issues are less spectacular and resemble a debating contest, the scene consisting of two attorneys presenting their arguments before a judge.

Let us now return to our seats in the courtroom and take note of the roles to be played by the various participants. The fact that a jury is present indicates that the trial will be concerned with factual issues, for the sole function of a jury is to determine the facts. When a trial involving factual issues is held without a jury, the determination of facts becomes part of the functions exercised by a judge. If by constitutional provision the parties, in a civil case, are entitled to a jury trial, either party may demand it. If neither party desires a jury trial, the trial is held without a jury. The United States Constitution governs this matter in Federal cases. State constitutions govern in state cases.

A judge presides over the proceeding, seeing to it that procedural rules are adhered to, rendering decisions on procedural issues that arise during the course of the trial, pronouncing to the jury the substantive rules of law applicable to the case, charging the jury with the bases upon which its verdict is to be reached, and finally announcing the judgment of the court. Of course, where the trial is held without a jury, the responsibilities of the judge are enlarged (finding the facts), while his exhortations are curtailed (no charge to the jury).

The attorneys have been retained to represent the respective parties and to manage their affairs during the process of litigation. The one will attempt to convince the jury that certain events have taken place, while the other will attempt to show the contrary. The establishment of facts depends upon the production of evidence through eyewitnesses, documents, or circumstances. Whatever the nature of the evidence, it will be introduced by the answers to questions propounded to witnesses by one of the attorneys. The other attorney will attempt, through cross-examination of those witnesses, to discredit evidence produced. There are rules within which the attorneys must operate in the production of evidence and, when one detects an infraction by the other, an objection is raised. The judge must then decide whether to sustain or overrule the objection. If he sustains the objection, the attorney who objected will be pleased, the other may take exception (note his disagreement with the ruling, thereby creating a legal issue to be decided later if there is an appeal taken to a higher court following the present proceeding) . If he overrules the objection, the attorney who objected may take exception. Before the production of evidence begins, attorneys make opening statements to the jury in order to acquaint the jury with what each side intends to establish. After all the evidence is in, the attorneys make closing statements in order to piece together the strands of evidence developed and to hammer home in the minds of the jurors that what had been set out to be demonstrated has been demonstrated.

The outcome of a trial depends upon two main factors: (1) the evidence produced; and (2) the recital of the law by the judge to the jury. The evidence produced depends upon the witnesses available, the rulings on objections, and the skill of the attorney. The recital of the law depends upon the knowledge and skill of the judge, as well as upon his acceptance or refusal of suggestions by the respective attorneys.

Objections to proffered evidence may be made on the grounds that such evidence is irrelevant, immaterial, or incompetent. To say that it is irrelevant is to say that it does not relate to the case. To say that it is immaterial is to say that, while it may relate to the case, it is not of sufficient weight to have a bearing on the outcome of the case. To say that it is incompetent is to say that the rules pertaining to the introduction of evidence do not allow its admission. Thus, it is plain to see that rulings by which evidence is admitted or excluded may have a distinct effect upon the final outcome, for the jury must consider only the evidence admitted.

Of equal importance with the establishment of the facts is the correctness of the statements made by the judge concerning the law to be applied. Although the jury may have the facts clearly in mind, even a slight misstatement of the law may lead to a verdict entirely different from that which may have been reached through the application of a correct version of the law.

If we stay long enough to see the entire performance, this is perhaps what we shall see. Each attorney will make his opening statement to the jury. The plaintiff's attorney will then call his first witness. He will subject the witness to a series of questions designed to elicit constructive evidence. The defendant's attorney will then subject the witness to a series of questions designed to create doubt as to the credibility of the witness, or to destroy the value of his testimony through the elicitation of admissions and contradictions. Objections are inevitable as the questioning proceeds, rulings will be made, and exceptions will be noted. Then another witness will take the stand, then another, and still another, until the plaintiff's list of witnesses is exhausted. Plaintiff's attorney will then announce: "Your Honor, the plaintiff rests." At this point, only the uninitiate will be surprised to hear the defendant's attorney make a motion to the effect that the case be dismissed on the ground that the plaintiff has failed to produce evidence sufficient to substantiate his complaint. If the judge feels that even a scintilla of evidence has been submitted (and he usually does), he will deny the motion. The defendant's attorney will then proceed to call his witnesses, who in turn will be subjected to direct and cross-examination. Objections again will interrupt the questioning, rulings will be made, and exceptions will be taken. Then will come the announcement: "Your Honor, the defendant rests." The defendant's attorney will then reiterate his previous motion, or make another to the effect that the judge direct the jury to return a verdict in favor of his client on the ground that his opponent has failed to provide any effective evidence for the jury to consider. The plaintiff's attorney will make a similar motion for direction of a verdict in favor of the plaintiff. If the judge agrees with either, he will direct the jury accordingly; otherwise, he will deny both motions. This will be followed by the closing statements of the attorneys to the jury. The attorneys may request that certain versions or expressions of the law be included by the judge in his charge to the jury. While the parties are resting, the judge turns to the jury and delivers an exposition on the law pertaining to the case, including or ignoring the requests of the attorneys. If the judge refuses to charge as requested, or if any portion of his charge is out of accord with the thinking of either attorney, an exception may be taken by such attorney. The jury will then retire for deliberation, sooner or later to return with a verdict. This will be followed by motions to set the verdict aside and to grant a new trial, or to render a judgment notwithstanding the verdict. If such motions are denied, judgment will be entered in accordance with the verdict.

The trial is now over, but is that the end of the case? Maybe yes, and maybe no. If the winner is satisfied with his winnings, and the loser is resigned to the fact of his loss, the case is history, except, of course, for the obligation of the loser to comply with the terms of the judgment. But if either party is dissatisfied with the result, may he not appeal?

Dissatisfaction alone is not a basis upon which to found an appeal. Remember the rulings made by the judge during the course of the trial? On objections? On motions? On requests to charge? And remember the charge to the jury made by the judge? These form the bedrock underlying appeals. Was there error upon the part of the judge in any of these? This is a question typical of those with which an appellate court is confronted. And remember the case in which the defendant demurs in his answer to the complaint? The decision on this legal issue is likewise appealable.

The scene shifts then to the appellate court. Here we find a panel of judges. The attorneys submit to this court briefs in which are outlined the appealable points at issue, together with arguments and citations of cases in support of the respective contentions. At an appointed time, the attorneys engage in oral argument before the panel and parry the thrusts of questions posed by the judges to test the strengths of the arguments. Some time later, after the judges have had the opportunity to make a thorough study of the points of law involved and to discuss the case among themselves, a decision will be reached by vote of the panel. The view of the majority will prevail, and one of that number will write and orally deliver the opinion of the court. Any other member of the majority may render an opinion, usually concurring in result but differing in line of reasoning. The minority views may be expressed in dissenting opinions. All these opinions will later appear in law reports placed upon the shelves of private and public law libraries, open to the inspection of all who care to examine them. It may be noted in passing that the dissenting opinions of today may constitute the views of the majority tomorrow.

There is no appeal beyond a court of last resort. The United States Supreme Court is such a court with regard to Federal matters and matters giving rise to an issue involving the United States Constitution. Matters categorized as consisting of strictly state affairs are appealable no further than to the highest court of the state.

To know the law is to know its aims, its modes of operation, and its fulfillments.

3

House of Privacy

The origin of rights lies in the treatment of human conduct and behavior by the body politic. Some actions are applauded and encouraged; others are derided and condemned. What determines the delineation between actions allowed and actions prohibited? Such determination cannot ignore the direct and indirect effects of deeds upon the individual and upon society. What man is willing to suffer encroachments upon his existence, his freedom of movement and expression, his physical well being, his peace of mind, his worldly possessions, his reputation, his business and social relationships, and may we add, his privacy? And what man is willing to stand by and to witness the practice of such encroachments when they are being experienced by another? Superficially, it seems that the answers to questions such as these are unequivocal. Nevertheless, closer examination will reveal that there are numerous implications to be considered: the relationship between individual and individual; the relationship between the individual and his community; the relationship between his community and other communities; the interests, aims and expectations of the individual as they are in consonance with, or in conflict with, those of other individuals or of the community; and the infinite variety of forms in which may be found the activities, in favor of which man seeks sanction, and against which man seeks protection.

Where a determination is dependent upon the consideration of several interests, whether they be harmonious or discordant, compromise is inevitable. Neither can the totality of a boon or bounty be given at one and the same time to each of many, nor can we in good conscience summarily deny any one of many who may be deserving. We cannot, moreover, disregard the rights of one man in enforcing the rights of another, nor can we overlook the rights of the group in upholding the rights of the individual, nor give undue preference to the interests of the community in evaluating the aspirations of the individual. Compromise means sacrifice. And sacrifice with respect to rights means limitations.

Even of the right to life itself it may be said that there are limitations. Not only may it be taken away in the form of punishment, but it may also be subjected to the hazards of the battlefield, a point from which only the fortunate return.

Is the right to freedom of movement absolute? Ask those involved in emigration and immigration. Ask the traveler to distant lands, the hunter, the fisherman, the swimmer, the automobile driver, the pedestrian, the canvasser, the schoolboy, the draftee. Ask the prisoner, the burglar, the robber, the thief, the arsonist, the trespasser, the parolee.

But is not the freedom of speech and freedom of the press guaranteed? Ask again the schoolboy, the spectator at a trial, the listener at a concert, the audible patron at a movie, the curbside orator, the domestic curser with fortissimo voice, the slanderer, the libeler, the infringer of copyrights, the revealer of trade secrets, the forger, the counterfeiter, the misbrander of labels, the false advertiser, the perjurer, the defrauder; ask especially the publisher, the writer, the editor, the public speaker, and the salesman. Let us not forget to ask those who teach the overthrow of government by force and violence, nor those who, in time of war, by their speaking and writing, seek to undermine the common effort.

Surely there is complete immunity in the right to corporal security! But no, we must not forget the battlefield, nor the child, nor the boxer, nor any other athlete, nor the unguarded spectator, nor the jaywalker, nor the careless driver, nor one who hurls the gauntlet of provocation, nor one who resists arrest or attempts to escape.

And may one ever with impunity disturb another's peace of mind? Think of a news report, a disappointing rejection, an unkind word, a failure to comply with a promise, an intentional or unintentional forebearance to give a gift or bestow a reward.

As to matters which one feels proud to call his own, his lands and buildings, his furniture and clothing, his stocks and bonds, his car, his boat, his bank account, his books and tools—are his rights with respect to these unlimited? One may find himself the unwilling seller of his lands and buildings upon a governmental exercise of its right of eminent domain. Zoning ordinances or previously negotiated restrictive covenants may alter his building plans or confine the uses to which the premises as presently constituted may be put. Only a bare subsistence portion of what he owns is immune from the impending claws of his unpaid creditors. He must always be careful to avoid transgressions upon the rights of others in using what he claims to be his property. He must not forget to pay the taxes levied against his property, else he will lose it. If he wishes to provide for the distribution of his property upon his death, not only must he leave a will which complies with the requirements of the law but, even then, not all may go as he wills it. If he leaves no will, his property will be distributed in accordance with the dictates of legislative enactments.

The favorable reputation of a person is one of his most highly prized attainments. Is his right to this treasured estimate also subject to limitations? The character of a man and his reputation may be wholly at variance with each other, since character resides within the framework of a person, while his reputation finds its abode within the minds of his fellowmen. Ideally, the two should coincide, but unfortunately, this is not always the case. A man cannot force others to think highly of him, nor can he prevent the deflation of an inflated esteem. Truth, even without justification for its utterance, and although a reputation may thereby be damaged, is in the majority of states allowed to stand as a complete defense against a claim of libel or slander. The occasional revelation of hitherto unknown or long forgotten misconduct on the part of one who has since established himself and his family among the pillars of a community is a familiar story. Then shall we conclude that all disparagements resulting from false statements are actionable? Oh no! The statements of judges, juries, attorneys, and witnesses, relevant to and made during court proceedings, are privileged, as are also the statements of the President, governors, members of Congress, and members of state legislatures, made in official capacities. The press is, moreover, privileged to publish such statements. It is not here intended to criticize, but merely to point out limitations to rights, with the hope that the reader may apply some thought toward discovering the reasons for what may on the surface appear to be unjust. Fair comment and criticism have certainly affected the reputations of individuals, such as office-holders, candidates for public office, actors, writers, and many others who submit their avowed talents to the discriminating tastes of the public. The public interest served in this regard by a free press is considered to outweigh the individual interest in an untarnished reputation.

Is man completely free in his business and social relationships? First of all, there are certain activities which are not allowed to be carried on without governmental license, such as the practice of law or medicine, real estate brokerage, pawn brokerage, barbering, electrical work, plumbing, saloon keeping, sale of liquors, banking, public utilities, insurance, to name a few. Labor legislation compels collective bargaining, minimum wages, maximum hours, safe and sanitary conditions, workmen's compensation. Prospective employees may be indirectly compelled to join unions in order to gain employment. The maintenance of a gambling establishment, except where permitted, is prohibited. Sunday laws curtail business activity. Antitrust laws modify the freedom of free enterprise. Usury laws limit the amount of interest chargeable on loans. And no one will doubt the distinctive effect of marriage and divorce laws upon rights with respect to social relationships.

What shall we say of privacy, first of the attributes claimed by man, last in point of recognition?

> And they were both naked, the man and his wife, and were not ashamed.
>
> .   .   .   .
>
> Now the serpent was more subtle than any beast of the field which the Lord God had made. And he said unto the woman: "Yea, hath God said: Ye shall not eat of any tree of the Garden." And the woman said unto the serpent: "Of the fruit of the trees of the garden we may eat; but of the fruit of the tree which is in the midst of the garden, God hath said: 'Ye shall not eat of it, neither shall ye touch it, lest ye die.' And the serpent said unto the woman: "Ye shall not surely die; for God doth know that in the day ye eat thereof, then your eyes shall be opened, and ye shall be as God, knowing good and evil." And when the woman saw that the tree was good for food, and that it was a delight to the eyes, and that the tree was to be desired to make one wise, she took of the fruit thereof, and did eat; and she gave also unto her husband with her, and he did eat. And the eyes of them both were opened, and they knew that they were naked; and they sewed fig-leaves together, and made themselves girdles. And the Lord God called unto the man, and said unto him: "Where art thou?" And he said: "I heard Thy voice in the garden, and I was afraid, because I was naked; and I hid myself . . ."
>
> .   .   .   .
>
> . . . And the Lord God made for Adam and for his wife garments of skins, and he clothed them. Genesis, 2:25-3:21.

Privacy involves more than freedom from the exposure of nakedness. Only in its simplest form has it been portrayed in the biblical story of Adam and Eve, but the account of its birth therein contained is symbolic of the claim each man makes to his individualism in an unindividualistic society. Like persecuted peoples who somehow survive periodic attempts to annihilate them, privacy persistently peers across the surface of engulfing waters, piercing the power of its opposition. Politicians proclaim the supremacy of the individual, then relegate him to the role of a puppet. One man pities another in distress, but exploits his predicament for monetary gain. One man guards his privacy while straining to satisfy his curiosity by indulgng in the affairs of others. Keep the home fires burning that they may provide light to guide the attentions of idle gossipers!

Considering the complexities and overpowering demands of current living, privacy assumes the appearance of an imaginary luxury. Few can afford it, but many cherish the idea of its availability. Can we separate that which one may keep to himself from that which one must allow to be exposed to others? If so, upon what considerations will the separation be made? As with all other legal determinations, all interests, conflicting or otherwise, must be considered. So far as privacy is concerned, the paramount interests which hover over the deliberations concerned with its treatment are those of the individual and those of the public.

Originally, men banded together for mutual protection. This did not mean the exploitation of individuals to benefit the group. Yet, some sacrifice is necessary on the part of individuals if any project is to succeed. Absolute freedom in one person means no freedom in any other. Freedom in society must be adjusted to the extent of providing for all such maximum allowances as will insure the same optimum level of freedom for all. This necessitates a balancing of interests in each case upon the scales of justice.

The searcher may find an occasional reference to privacy in cases decided before 1890, but today there is veritable agreement that, as currently conceived, the right of privacy owes its inception to the brilliance of an article published in that year. The article written by Samuel D. Warren and Louis D. Brandeis, entitled "The Right to Privacy" (4 *Harvard Law Review* 193), stands as a monument within whose shadow courts deliberate upon claims alleging transgressions of privacy. So seldom is mention of or quotation from this article neglected in the composition of court opinions dealing with this subject that we cannot, in approaching the house of privacy, hope to appreciate its interior without reading the inscription engraved upon its gate. The words are those of Warren and Brandeis:

> That the individual shall have full protection in person and in property is a principle as old as the common law; but it has been found necessary from time to time to define anew the exact nature and extent of such protection. Political, social, and economic changes entail the recognition of new rights, and the common law, in its eternal youth, grows to meet the demands of society. Thus, in very early times, the law gave a remedy only for physical interference with life and property . . . Then the "right to life" served only to protect the subject from battery in its various forms; liberty meant freedom from actual restraint; and the right to property secured to the individual his lands and his cattle. Later, there came a

recognition of man's spiritual nature, of his feelings and his intellect. Gradually the scope of these legal rights broadened; and now the right to life has come to mean the right to enjoy life—the right to be let alone; the right to liberty secures the exercise of extensive civil privileges; and the term "property" has grown to comprise every form of possession—intangible as well as tangible . . .

Warren and Brandeis felt the temper of the times. The questionable art of gossip in newspapers was running rampant. The individual was being exploited. Where was the full protection to which every person was entitled? Pain and suffering had been recognized as accompanying results of physical injuries. Reputations had been accorded monetary value. Published literary and artistic works had been given protection under the copyright laws. Unpublished works had also been recognized as worthy of protection, but upon theories so artificially applied that the true basis upon which such protection should have been founded was overlooked and neglected.

Suppose, for example, that A writes a letter to B. Does B have the right to publish the letter? Certainly not! But why not? Does A still own the letter? Is the letter A's property? Is there an agreement between A and B that B will not publish the letter? Has a trust been created so that B is a trustee? Can there be an agreement without the mutual assent of both parties? Can there be a trust without the consent of the intended trustee? Can one own that which he has voluntarily given away? And yet, as pointed out by Warren and Brandeis, the wrong committed by B in publishing the letter has been considered by the courts to be a breach of contract or trust, or the violation of a property right. The practical observer would say, "So what? What difference does it make upon what theory the wrong is requited so long as justice prevails?" The answer is that it would make no difference provided all wrongs of a similar nature were couched in similar circumstances. It so happened that earlier cases lent themselves to the application of contract and trust theories because, in each case, the victim had put something in the hands of another—a letter, a picture, or an etching. And, of course, if the same physical things had been stolen by a thief, there would be no doubt as to the applicability of property rights. However, there is more involved than just the physical thing. There is the personality of the victim, the right to be let alone, the right to privacy. What if the case does not lend itself to the construction of a contract, or a trust, or if no physical object has been stolen? How shall we deal with the indulgence in and the devulgence of private affairs? How shall we deal with exploitations of personality?

Time brings about changes, and the law must be broad enough to encompass such changes. Scientific, economic and social developments call for a fresh application of basic principles. Where justice could be achieved by concentrating on the physical things involved, it did not matter that the element of personality was disregarded. But when new devices make possible interferences with personality without the involvement of material matters owned by the victim, then personality must be given separate and distinct recognition. Warren and Brandeis put it this way:

> . . . The narrower doctrine may have satisfied the demands of society at a time when the abuse to be guarded against could rarely have arisen without violating a contract or a special confidence; but now that modern devices afford abundant opportunities for the perpetration of such wrongs without any participation by the injured party, the protection granted by the law must be placed upon a broader foundation . . . The right of property in its widest sense, including all possession, including all rights and privileges, and hence embracing the right to an inviolate personality, affords alone that broad basis upon which the protection which the individual demands can be rested.

We all have a tendency to lean heavily upon the past. It is general practice to define new concepts through the use of established terminology. This is especially true in the law. A novel idea is more readily acceptable if it can be made to fit within a fundamental category. And so Warren and Brandeis felt that if "the right to an inviolate personality" was not independently recognizable, the right of property, in its widest sense, should be visualized as including the concept of an inviolate personality. People do bargain away their services and productions; the exposure of their private affairs may also be for sale. But the authors were not satisfied that spiritual matters should be classified with material matters. They were determined that the right to an inviolate personality should have an independent standing. Thus they observed:

> . . . The principle which protects personal writings and all other personal productions, not against theft and physical appropriation, but against publication in any form, is in reality not the principle of private property but that of an inviolate personality.

When one is bent upon the acceptance by others of his ideas, knowing that compromise may mean an advance, he presents alternatives and stresses his preference. The right to an inviolate personality deserves recognition. If need be, let it be considered as a subdivision of the right to property. But if we are to be realistic we should recognize it for all that it is, not as a right to property, but as a right to privacy.

This is the conclusion reached by Warren and Brandeis:

> We must therefore conclude that the rights, so protected, whatever their exact nature, are not rights arising from contract or from special trust, but are rights as against the world; and, as above stated, the principle which has been applied to protect these rights is in reality not the principle of private property, unless that word be used in an extended and unusual sense. The principle which protects personal writings and any other productions of the intellect or of the emotions, is the right to privacy, and the law has no new principle to formulate when it extends this protection to the personal appearance, sayings, acts, and to personal relation, domestic or otherwise.

To sum up the thoughts expressed by Warren and Brandeis in their monumental essay, the following basic points should be noted: that the common law is not a closed chapter, but is constantly alive and growing together with the rest of civilization; that concepts of basic rights become broader as human activity becomes greater and intellect becomes more profound; that conservatism constrains men to confine their considerations within familiar boundaries; that such conservatism has caused courts to place all rights into established classifications even though some rights are virtually forced into pigeonholes, while other apparent rights are discarded with regret; that although privacy may involve property, its personality aspect should not be neglected; that the application of contract and trust theories to basically privacy cases is a fiction; and that no new principle is necessary for according full recognition to the right of privacy.

Lest there be question as to whether "right *to* privacy" or "right *of* privacy" is correct, let it be noted that, while Warren and Brandeis preferred the former expression, the latter has become the common expression used by courts and legislatures in matters involving privacy.

4

New York Reception

Having cast their offering upon the scales of justice, Warren and Brandeis stepped aside so that all might view its reception. Twelve years went by before the initial occasion for a full-dress reception arose.

The first case to reach a court of last resort following the publication of "The Right to Privacy" in the *Harvard Law Review* was entitled *Roberson v. Rochester Folding Box Co.* (1902), a New York case. The case arose upon the complaint that 25,000 lithographic prints, photographs and likenesses of the plaintiff, a girl, had been made, sold and circulated by the defendants; that above the picture of the plaintiff appeared the words "Flour of the Family," below it, "Franklin Mills Flour," and in the lower right hand corner, "Rochester Folding Box Co., Rochester, N. Y."; that this advertising matter was posted and displayed in stores, warehouses, saloons, and other public places; that friends recognizing plaintiff in such portrayal scoffed and jeered, causing her humiliation, distress, and suffering, both mental and physical; that, stricken with severe nervous shock, plaintiff was under the care of a physician. Basing her case upon the theory that her privacy had been and was being invaded, plaintiff asked for an injunction to stop the continued publication of her picture, and for damages in the amount of $15,000.

In evaluating the claim asserted, let us bear in mind that this was a young girl, presumably attractive, from whom no permission to use her photography in the manner above described had been solicited. And, needless to say, no such permission had ever been granted. Assuming the truth of the allegations, would you consider the plaintiff to have been wronged in any way? Well, we shall see what happened.

In answer to the complaint, the defendants asserted that the plaintiff had failed to state a cause of action. This meant that the only issue to be decided was whether or not there was any legal basis upon which a decision favorable to the plaintiff could be rendered. The plaintiff contended that there existed a right known as the right of privacy, and that a statement of facts showing a violation of such right was a statement of a cause of action. The defendants contended that there was no such thing in the law as a right of privacy. And so the case revolved around the issue as to whether or not, according to the laws of the State of New York, there existed such right as was claimed by the plaintiff.

The state court system in New York is built upon three levels: the lowest is the Trial Division of the Supreme Court; the second is the Appellate Division of the Supreme Court; and the highest is the Court of Appeals. Where the legal issue is hotly contested, one cannot safely begin counting chickens until a decision at the highest level has been rendered.

The plaintiff and the defendants presented their arguments at a Special Term of the Supreme Court and, after carefully weighing the *pros* and *cons,* the court decided in favor of the plaintiff. The right of privacy was thus accorded recognition. But the defendants did not give up. They took the case to the Appellate Division, and this higher court put its stamp of approval on the decision of the lower court. It was beginning to look as though the right of privacy would at last be given complete recognition. But the defendants were persistent. They went to the Court of Appeals, a court having seven members on its panel of judges. What future course the law would take with respect to privacy hung in the balance as these seven judges listened to arguments and then retired to deliberate.

When the smoke of battle had cleared away, there lay the right of privacy—buried beneath the weight of four majority votes. What had looked like a sure victory was turned to a disappointing defeat by the measure of one vote.

Chief Judge Parker delivered the opinion of the court:

> There is no precedent for such an action to be found in the decisions of this court . . .

The line of reasoning followed by the majority was that never before had the Court of Appeals decided a case in favor of a plaintiff on the .theory that a right of privacy had been invaded. Why, even the judge who rendered the opinion for the Appellate Division admitted that the theory was new, "at least in instance if not in principle," and that no authoritative cases could be found to sustain the position taken by the plaintiff. And yet, despite the lack of precedent, that court found in favor of the plaintiff on the ground that the plaintiff's right of privacy had been invaded. Blackstone, the authority on English law, and Kent, the authority on American law, had never mentioned such a right, nor had any other of the great commentators. Who ever heard of such a right before 1890? Warren and Brandeis did a remarkable job, but the adoption and application of their views by this court would not be feasible.

Judge Parker envisioned the claimed right in this way:

> The so-called right of privacy is, as the phrase suggests, founded upon the claim that a man has the right to pass through this world, if he wills, without having his picture published, his business enterprises discussed, his successful experiments written up for the benefit of others, or his eccentricities commented upon either in handbills, circulars, catalogues, periodicals or newspapers, and, necessarily, that the things which may not be written and published of him must not be spoken of him by his neighbors, whether the comment be favorable or otherwise . . .

Taking an exaggerated view of the proposition, as though a court had no discretion in discerning between worthy and unworthy claims, the learned judge likewise viewed with alarm the possible consequences of its adoption:

> If such a principle be incorporated into the body of the law through the instrumentality of a court of equity, the attempts to logically apply the principle will necessarily result, not only in a vast amount of litigation, but in litigation bordering upon the absurd, for the right of privacy, once established as a legal doctrine, cannot be confined to the restraint of the publication of a likeness but must necessarily embrace as well the publication of a word-picture, a comment upon one's looks, conduct, domestic relations or habits. And were the right of privacy once legally asserted it would necessarily be held to include the same things if spoken instead of printed, for one, as well as the other, invades the right to be absolutely let alone. An insult would certainly be in violation of such a right and with many persons would more seriously wound the feelings than would the publication of their picture . . .

The court was afraid that once the recognition of privacy was asserted, although it be asserted in a case which seemed to warrant such assertion, every conceivable claim involving privacy would find its way into the courts. The majority felt that the principle of privacy needed dissection, and that the proper instrumentality for such purpose was the legislature:

> The legislative body could very well interfere and arbitrarily provide that no one should be permitted for his own selfish purpose to use the picture or the name of another for advertising purposes without his consent. In such event no embarrassment would result to the general body of the law, for the rule would be applicable only to cases provided for by the statute. The courts, however, being without authority to legislate, are required to decide cases upon principle, and so are necessarily embarrassed by precedents created by an extreme, and, therefore, unjustifiable application of an old principle.

What did this mean? Were courts confined to moderate applications of established principles? Did principles have meaningless limits? Was the court conceding that there was a principle embracing privacy, but contending that its application in this case would be ex-
treme? As Judge Parker went on with his opinion, he agreed with the
Appellate Division that want of a precedent was not a sufficient reason for turning a plaintiff out of court, but with the proviso that "there
can be found a clear and unequivocal principle of the common law"
governing the case. The trouble was, however, that he was looking
for a principle in precedents and, having found no precedents, he concluded that such principle was nonexistent. According to his view,
formulated on the basis of observations expressed by Pomeroy, an
eminent authority on the law, the body of equitable principles, doctrines and rules had long ago ceased to grow:

> It is undoubtedly true that in the early days of chancery jurisdiction in
> England, the chancellors were accustomed to deliver their judgments with-
> out regard to principles or precedents and in that way the process of
> building up the system of equity went on, the chancellor disregarding
> absolutely many established principles of the common law. "In no other
> way," says Pomeroy, "could the system of equity jurisprudence have been
> commenced and continued so as to arrive at its present proportions."
> (Pomeroy's Eq. Jur. sec. 48). In their work the chancellors were guided
> not only by what they regarded as the eternal principles of absolute right,
> but also by their individual consciences, but after a time when "the period
> of infancy was passed and an orderly system of equitable principles, doc-
> trines and rules began to be developed out of the increasing mass of prece-
> dents, this theory of a personal conscience was abandoned; and "the con-
> science," which is an element of the equitable jurisdiction, came to be
> regarded and has continued to the present day, as a metaphorical term,
> designating the common standard of civil right and expediency combined,
> based upon general principles and limited by established doctrines to
> which the court appeals, and by which it tests the conduct and rights of
> suitors—a juridical and not a personal conscience." (Pomeroy's Eq. Jur.
> sec. 57).

Conceding that justice in a particular case might best be achieved
through a decision dictated by the conscience of an individual judge
or body of judges, Judge Parker felt it more important to guard against
the mischief that would inevitably result from such practice. It was
his feeling that to uphold the right of privacy in the present case would
be to step beyond the beaten paths of both common law and equity,
thus inviting danger.

To demonstrate his point that the right of privacy had not been
established as a legal doctrine, the learned judge reviewed past Eng-

lish decisions based upon theories of property, contract, and trust, rather than upon the theory of an inviolate personality as urged by Warren and Brandeis. Let us look at some of these cases.

Prince Albert v. Strange. Prince Albert and his wife, Queen Victoria, having made some etchings and drawings, employed a workman to make some copies. As sometimes happens, the workman made extra copies for himself, and they found their way into the hands of a stranger named Strange, who, wishing to exhibit them for profit, published a descriptive catalogue. An injunction was granted against the exhibition and the catalogue.

Pollard v. Photographic Co. The plaintiff sat for a picture and, as usually happens, ordered copies to be made. Instead of making the number ordered, the photographer made extras, exhibited them, and then sold copies to a stationer who used them as Christmas cards. The defendant was enjoined from using the negative except to make copies for the plaintiff.

Gee v. Pritchard. An attempt to print and publish a private letter received from another was enjoined.

Abernathy v. Hutchinson. The publication, by a student, of a lecture delivered by the plaintiff was enjoined.

Mayhall v. Higbey. The plaintiff loaned some negatives to a person who later became insolvent. The assignee who was appointed for the benefit of his creditors sold the negatives to the defendant, who proceeded to print and sell copies. An injunction was granted against this practice.

Duke of Queensbury v. Shebbeare. The Earl of Clarendon delivered to one Gwynne an original manuscript of his father's *Lord Clarendon's History.* When Gwynne died, the administrator of his estate sold the manuscript to the defendant, who wished to publish the work. Lord Clarendon being dead, his personal representatives sued for an injunction to stop the publication. The injunction was granted.

For one acquainted with dyed-in-the-wool legalistic thinking, it is relatively simple to detect property and contract aspects in the situations related above. However, especially in a case such as the one involving the receipt of a personal letter, as Warren and Brandeis tried to point out, it is difficult to find a property or contract aspect. And a court, feeling constrained to follow the beaten path, distorts a concept in yielding to a sense of justice, rather than to effectuate hitherto unfamiliar principles. Thus, Judge Parker continues:

> In not one of these cases, therefore, was it the basis of the decision that the defendant could be restrained from performing the act he was doing

or threatening to do on the ground that the feelings of the plaintiff would be thereby injured; but, on the contrary, each decision was rested either upon the ground of breach of trust or that plaintiff had a property right in the subject of litigation which the court could protect.

The opinion then dealt with a more recent English case which seemed to be more in point.

Dockrell v. Dougall. The defendant, in advertising a medicine called "Sallyco," published the following substantially true but unauthorized statement: "Dr. Morgan Dockrell, physician to St. John's Hospital, London, is prescribing Sallyco as an habitual drink. Dr. Dockrell says nothing has done his gout so much good." In denying an injunction the court said that only such use of a name as causes injury to reputation or property would be enjoined.

The court then turned to American decisions, speaking first to a case on which it seemed the Appellate Division had heavily relied.

Schuyler v. Curtis. Certain persons wished to erect a statue or bust of a woman no longer living. One of her relatives sought to restrain such erection, claiming that his feelings, as well as the feelings of other relatives, would be injured by the contemplated action. The New York Court of Appeals reversed the lower court decision which had granted an injunction. The court spoke of privacy, stating that it was not denying the existence of a right of privacy, but found it unnecessary to apply such a principle to the case before it.

Judge Parker pointed out that whatever favorable light may appear to have been shed upon the doctrine of privacy by the Schuyler case was not authority for the position taken by the plaintiff in the present case. Whenever the remarks contained in a judicial opinion venture beyond the precise question to be decided, such remarks are referred to as dicta, mere words having no effect as points of law.

Two more New York cases were then discussed, both of which had been decided on the first floor level, with no appeal taken.

Marks v. Jaffa. The plaintiff was an actor, and at the time of the action was a law school student. There was another actor by the name of Mogulesko, who was equally well known. The defendant was editor of a newspaper called *Der Wachter.* This editor thought of the idea of publishing the pictures of the two actors and inviting the public to vote for their preference, thus to prove which of the two was the more popular. Plaintiff declined to give his consent, but defendant proceeded with his plan anyway. In granting an injunction the court said:

An individual is entitled to protection in person as well as property, and now the right to life has come to mean the privilege to enjoy life without the publicity or annoyance of a lottery contest waged without authority, on the result of which is made to depend, in public estimation at least, the worth of private character or value of ability.

Judge Parker observed that the Marks case had been decided on the basis of the lower court decision in the Schuyler case which, as noted above, was later reversed by the Court of Appeals.

Murray v. Gast Lithographic and Engraving Co. A parent sought to enjoin the publication of an infant child's portrait and to recover damages for injury to the parent's sensibilities caused by the invasion of the child's privacy. After saying that "the law takes no cognizance of a sentimental injury, independent of a wrong to person or property," the court went on to quote from *Chapman v. Western Union Telegraph Co.,* an old Georgia case:

> The law protects the person and the purse. The person includes the reputation. The body, reputation and property of the citizen are not to be invaded without responsibility in damages to the sufferer. But, outside these protected spheres, the law does not yet attempt to guard the peace of mind, the feelings or the happiness of everyone by giving recovery of damages for mental anguish produced by mere negligence. There is no right, capable of enforcement by process of law, to possess or maintain, without disturbance, any particular condition of feeling. The law leaves feeling to be helped and vindicated by the tremendous force of sympathy. The temperaments of individuals are various and variable, and the imagination exerts a powerful and incalculable influence in injuries of this kind. There are many moral obligations too delicate and subtle to be enforced in the rude way of giving money compensation for their violation. Perhaps the feelings find as full protection as it is possible to give in moral law and a responsive public opinion. The civil law is a practical business system, dealing with what is tangible, and does not undertake to redress psychological injuries.

Having dealt with previous English and New York decisions, Judge Parker then returned to cases decided in other jurisdictions.

Corliss v. E. W. Walker Co. This action was commenced in a Federal District Court in Massachusetts. It involved an attempt to restrain the publication of a biography and picture of George H. Corliss, an inventor, on the ground that such publication would be an invasion of the right of privacy. At first, only the prayer for an injunction concerning the biography was denied, but later, on motion to dissolve the injunction granted with reference to the picture, the portion of relief theretofore given was withdrawn. The reason? Mr. Corliss was a "public character." Said the court:

I believe the law to be that a private individual has a right to be protected in the representation of his portrait in any form; that this is a property as well as a personal right, and that it belongs to the same class of rights which forbids the reproduction of a private manuscript or painting, or the publication of private letters, or of oral lectures delivered by a teacher to his class, or the revelation of the contents of a merchant's book by a clerk . . . But, while the right of a private individual to prohibit the reproduction of his picture or photograph should be recognized and enforced, this right may be surrendered or dedicated to the public by the act of the individual, just the same as a private manuscript, book or painting becomes (when not protected by copyright) public property by the act of publication. The distinction in the case of a picture or photograph lies, it seems to me, between public and private characters. A private individual should be protected against the publication of any portrait of himself, but where an individual becomes a public character the case is different. A statesman, author, artist or inventor, who asks for and desires public recognition, may be said to have surrendered his right to the public.

Insofar as the decision in the Corliss case denied relief it was regarded with approval by Judge Parker, but in its discussion of a distinction between public and private characters the learned judge found "a fatal objection to the establishment of a rule of privacy." Said Judge Parker:

The distinction between public and private characters cannot possibly be drawn. On what principle does an author or artist forfeit his right of privacy and a great orator, a great preacher, or a great advocate retain his? Who can draw a line of demarcation between public characters and private characters, let that line be as wavering and irregular as you please? In the very case then before the judge, what had Mr. Corliss done by which he surrendered his right of privacy? In what respect did he by his inventions "ask for and desire public recognition" any more than a banker or merchant who prosecutes his calling? Or is the right of privacy the possession of mediocrity alone, which a person forfeits by giving rein to his ability, spurs to his industry or grandeur to his character? A lady may pass her life in domestic privacy when, by some act of heroism or self-sacrifice, her name and fame fill the public ear. Is she to forfeit by her good deed the right of privacy she previously possessed? These considerations suggest the answer we would make to the position of the learned judge and at the same time serve to make more clear what we have elsewhere attempted to point out, namely, the absolute impossibility of dealing with this subject save by legislative enactment, by which may be drawn arbitrary distinctions which no court could promulgate as a part of general jurisprudence.

Well, such words certainly supply food for thought. One can almost feel in their expression the pounding of the craftsman as he puts his hammer to the nail. Yes, how does one distinguish between a public and a private character? And yet, is the difficulty of distinction a sufficient reason for denying justice? Are "arbitrary" distinctions, products of whim and caprice, more satisfactory when promulgated by legislatures? Does not due process of law prohibit arbitrary legislation? Later, we shall see the blurry lines of legislative demarcation. For the moment, let us turn to a Michigan decision, with which Judge Parker found himself in complete agreement.

Atkinson v. Doherty. Colonel John Atkinson, a well-known lawyer in Detroit, was dead. The defendant, a cigar manufacturer, used the colonel's name and portrait on his cigar boxes. The colonel's widow, being displeased with this procedure (as who will deny that she might be), sued for an injunction to put a stop to this practice. The relief prayed for was denied, and the decision of the lower court was affirmed on appeal. Said the Supreme Court of Michigan:

> This law of privacy seems to have gained a foothold at one time in the history of our jurisprudence—not by that name it is true—but in effect. It is evidenced by the old maxim, "the greater the truth the greater the libel," and the result has been the emphatic expression of public disapproval, by the emancipation of the press and the establishment of freedom of speech, and the abolition in most of the states of the maxim quoted by constitutional provisions. The limitations upon the exercise of these rights being the law of slander and libel, whereby the publication of an untruth that can be presumed or shown to the satisfaction, not of the plaintiff, but of others (i.e., an impartial jury), to be injurious, not alone to the feelings, but to the reputation, is actionable. Should it be thought that it is a hard rule that is applied in this case, it is only necessary to call attention to the fact that a ready remedy is to be found in legislation. We are not satisfied, however, that the rule is a hard one, and think that the consensus of opinion must be that the complainants contend for a much harder one. The law does not remedy all evils. It cannot, in the nature of things; and deliberation may well be used in considering the propriety of an innovation such as this case suggests. We do not wish to be understood as belittling the complaint. We have no reason to doubt the feeling of annoyance alleged. Indeed, we sympathize with it, and marvel at the impertinence which does not respect it. We can only say that it is one of the ills that under the law cannot be redressed.

. . . .

> An examination of the authorities leads us to the conclusion that the so-called "right of privacy" has not as yet found an abiding place in our jurisprudence, and, as we view it, the doctrine cannot now be incorporated without doing violence to settled principles of law by which the profession and the public have long been guided.

The concluding paragraph is a reminder that the law of libel is still available to provide a remedy for the unauthorized circulation of a likeness if it is a "malicious publication by picture, effigy or sign which exposes a person to contempt, ridicule or obloquy."

Judge Gray delivered a dissenting opinion, concurred in by two of his colleagues. Let us examine some excerpts from that opinion. The first is a retort to the treatment accorded to the Schuyler case by Judge Parker:

> The existence of the individual's right to be protected against the invasion of his privacy, if not actually affirmed in the opinion, was, very certainly, far from being denied. "It may be admitted," Judge Peckham observed, when delivering the opinion of the court, "that courts have power, in some cases, to enjoin the doing of an act, where the nature, or character, of the act itself is well calculated to wound the sensibilities of an individual, and where the doing of the act is wholly unjustifiable, and is, in legal contemplation, a wrong, even though the existence of no property, as that term is usually used, is involved in the subject."
>
> That the individual has a right of privacy, which he can enforce and which equity will protect against the invasion of, is a proposition which is not opposed by any decision in this court and which, in my opinion, is within the field of accepted legal principles.
>
> .   .   .   .
>
> The right of privacy, or the right of the individual to be let alone, is a personal right, which is not without judicial recognition. It is the complement of the right to the immunity of one's person. The individual has always been entitled to be protected in the exclusive use and enjoyment of that which is his own. The common law regarded his person and property as inviolate, and he has the absolute right to be let alone. . . . The principle is fundamental and essential in organized society that every one, in exercising a personal right and in the use of his property, shall respect the rights and property of others. He must so conduct himself, in the enjoyment of the rights and privileges which belong to him as a member of society, as that he shall prejudice no one in the possession and enjoyment of those which are exclusively his. When, as here, there is an alleged invasion of some personal right, or privilege, the absence of exact precedent and the fact that early commentators upon the common law have no discussion upon the subject are of no material importance in awarding equitable relief. That the exercise of the preventive power of a court of equity is demanded in a novel case, is not a fatal objection. . . . In the social evolution, with the march of the arts and sciences and in the resultant effects upon organized society, it is quite intelligible that new conditions must arise in personal relations, which the rules of the common law, cast in the rigid mould of an earlier social status, were not designed to meet. It would be a reproach to equitable jurisprudence, if equity were powerless to extend the application of the principles of common law, or of natural justice, in remedying a wrong, which, in the prog-

ress of civilization, has been made possible as the result of new social, or commercial conditions.

. . . .

. . . Sir Henry Maine, in his work on Ancient Law, has observed of equity, that it is an agency "by which law is brought into harmony with society," and that it is one of the factors, which operate in judicial evolution. It succeeds legal fictions, or those judicial assumptions, through which a rule of law is modified in its operation, and it precedes legislation. (See *Maine's Ancient Law,* pp. 22 to 28). Equity has neither fixed boundaries, nor logical subdivisions and its origin, both in Rome and in England, was that there was a wrong for which there was no remedy at law. (See 1st Story *Eq. Juris.* secs. 49 and 50). It supplements the deficiencies of the common law, by applying, where otherwise there would result a wrong, those principles of natural justice, which are analogous to settled principles of the common law. (See Story's Eq. Jur. sec. 671, note.)

. . . .

The right to grant the injunction does not depend upon the existence of property, which one has in some contractual form. It depends upon the existence of property in any right which belongs to a person.

And so the case came to an end, and the claim to relief and redress for an invasion of the right of privacy was denied. While some might with complacency contend that no great harm had been done, it cannot be gainsaid that a wrong had been committed. To say that a victim has not been wronged is to say that the culprit has acted within his rights. And who is to judge the importance of a case? "Equal Justice Under The Law" is the lettering that appears above the columns fronting the Supreme Court building. This means not only that the same law will be applied to all who come before the bar of justice, but also that the same judicial vigor will be exercised in the evaluation of claims, be they humble or lofty. To say that vigor was lacking in the Roberson case would be to contradict the truth, but to say that justice was done would be to insult a conscientious mentality. The main contention of the majority was that there was no precedent. The main contention of the minority was that lack of a precedent should not operate so as to deprive a party of his just dessert. The majority felt that it was up to the legislature to determine what treatment should be accorded similar cases in the future. The minority felt that wherever a wrong is discovered a remedy should be provided. The majority was fearful of increased litigation. If such reasoning were followed in automobile accident cases, who would dare predict the unimaginable chaos?

The Roberson case presented but one instance out of many in which persons have pointed to invasions of privacy and, although it granted to the aggrieved party no relief, it aroused public resentment, and the legislature in Albany went to work. We shall presently deal with the resulting legislation, but we shall not later neglect to deal with the ever increasing threats to individual liberty and the ever decreasing scope of personal immunity. The Roberson case dealt with the use of a picture, without authority, for advertising purposes, but we shall see that there are many other invasions of privacy complained of, such as newspaper stories, magazine stories, novels, biographies, motion pictures, fingerprinting, radio broadcasting, televising, shadowing, eavesdropping, tape recording, wire tapping, searches and seizures, questionable methods used to collect debts and, of course, intrusion into private quarters. Only those who have felt the whip of invasion know the effect of its sting, but let others beware lest the whip find its mark in places hitherto considered beyond the bounds of imagination.

5

A Line of Demarcation

Following the decision in the Roberson case, the New York legislature worked feverishly to plug a gap made obvious by the majority opinion in that case. Judge Parker had suggested that a legislature was the proper agency for promulgating arbitrary lines of demarcation, and so the representatives of the people took up the challenge. In 1903, two sections were added to the Civil Rights Law, and there was inserted as a title above these sections the heading, "Right of Privacy." The first of the two has never been amended; the second was amended in 1911, and again in 1921. These, then, are the sections of the law on which the right of privacy is made to depend in New York State. Herein has been set a line of demarcation. The language seems to set the line perfectly, but experience in application often reveals uncontemplated difficulties. Let us first have a look at these sections, and then we shall observe their applications.

Section 50: A person, firm or corporation that uses for advertising purposes, or for the purposes of trade, the name, portrait or picture of any living person without having first obtained the written consent of such person, or if a minor of his or her parent or guardian, is guilty of a misdemeanor.

Section 51: Any person whose name, portrait or picture is used within this state for advertising purposes or for the purposes of trade without the written consent first obtained as above provided may maintain an equitable action in the Supreme Court of this state against the person, firm or corporation so using his name, portrait or picture, to prevent and restrain the use thereof; and may also sue and recover damages for any injuries sustained by reason of such use and if the defendant shall have knowingly used such person's name, portrait or picture in such manner as is forbidden or declared to be unlawful by the last section, the jury, in its discretion, may award exemplary damages. But nothing contained in this act shall be so construed as to prevent any person, firm or corporation, practicing the profession of photography, from exhibiting in or about his or its establishment specimens of the work of such establishment, unless the same is continued by such person, firm or corporation after written notice objecting thereto has been given by the person portrayed; and nothing contained in this act shall be so construed as to prevent any person, firm or corporation from using the name, portrait or picture of any manufacturer or dealer in connection with the goods, wares and merchandise manufactured, produced or dealt in by

41

him which he has sold or disposed of with such name, portrait or picture used in connection therewith; or from using the name, portrait or
picture of any author, composer or artist in connection with his literary,
musical or artistic productions which he has sold or disposed of with
such name, portrait or picture used in connection therewith.

It is impossible to say with any degree of accuracy how many times
section 50 has been violated since its enactment, nor how many instances have arisen under which section 51 has been available. Not all
persons whose rights are invaded take advantage of the remedies provided by law. Some cases fall short of full dress proceedings through
the instrumentality of settlement. Furthermore, not all the results of
court proceedings are found in the law reports. Yet, the wealth of
material reported has given us a sufficient clue as to the status of privacy
in New York State.

It is almost inevitable that new legislation will sooner or later be
subjected to the test of its constitutional validity. Sometimes enactments are deliberately violated in order to hasten the test. Whether
by design or otherwise, sections 50 and 51 were put to the test in 1908.

Rhodes v. Sperry and Hutchinson Co. Everyone is familiar with the
business promotion device of giving to customers red, blue, green, or
perhaps brown stamps, the number depending upon the value of a
purchase, and providing for their redemption upon the selection of
some article by the customer. The defendant was in the business of
issuing and redeeming such stamps, and, for such purpose, occupied
premises in New York City and there exhibited premiums from which
customers made their selection. Among the premiums exhibited was
a series of pictures depicting the plaintiff in various poses. The plaintiff brought action under section 51, and the defendant contended that
the enactment did not represent a valid exercise of the legislative
power granted by the New York Constitution in that, as defendant
said, it deprived persons of liberty and property without due process of
law. It was further contended that the statute impaired the obligation
of contracts in violation of the United States Constitution.

The trial court issued an injunction against the use of plaintiff's
pictures, by the defendant, for advertising or trade purposes, and
awarded plaintiff $1,000 in damages. An appeal was taken to the
Appellate Division on the constitutional issue, and the decision of
that body affirming the judgment of the lower court was later affirmed
by the Court of Appeals.

The Court of Appeals gave answers to the contentions of constitutional violations set forth by the defendant. As to the assertion that

the statute deprived persons of liberty, the court said that the only liberty that might be involved would be that of a person to use his own portrait, and no one was denying him that right; further, that in order to conceive of another's liberty as being involved we would have to assume an inherent right in the public at large to use the portraits of individuals, without consent, for advertising or trade purposes. As to the question of interference with property, the court said that the statute did not apply to pictures in which another had acquired a property right before the enactment, but that the effect of the statute, in this regard, was to negative for the future any implication that the mere transfer of ownership in a picture gave a right to its use, without written authority, for advertising or trade purposes. As to interference with contracts, the court rhetorically asked how the statute could possibly interfere with contracts which were nonexistent at the time of the enactment. And finally, as to the contention that the legislature had abused its power, the court had this to say:

> The power of the Legislature, in the absence of any constitutional restriction, to declare that a particular act shall constitute a crime, or be actionable as a tort, cannot be questioned, where the right established, or recognized and sought to be protected, is based upon an ethical sanction.

Now that the constitutional deck had been cleared, the stage was set for a closer look at the product of New York legislative action. There was need for interpretation. The prohibition was directed at the use of names, portraits and pictures, of living persons for *advertising or trade purposes.* Conceivably, cases might involve questions as to the intended meaning of any one or more of these terms, but for the most part questions that arose were concerned with an imaginary line of demarcation, separating the use for advertising or trade purposes from all other uses. This became more evident as time went on, but even more evident became the fact that the association of the title, "Right of Privacy," with the substance of sections 50 and 51 was not fully congruous. The enactment struck down the commercialization of privacy, but left untouched the concept of an inviolate personality. And even as to the commercial aspect there arose a questionable interpretative delineation between a commercial and a non-commercial use.

It was clear from the beginning that any unauthorized use of a name or picture of a person in advertising matter, or the unauthorized use of a person's photograph or portrait as an article of trade, or a false representation that a person had endorsed or had had some connection with an article of trade, would be treated as unlawful. There could be no doubt that the legislature had aimed to prevent a recurrence of the injustice resulting from the *Roberson* decision. The question as to whether or not the statute had been violated in the *Rhodes* case presented no problem at all. Later cases involving articles of trade have been dealt with in comparatively routine fashion.

In *Garden v. Parfumerie Rigaud* (1933), it was held that Mary Garden, the famous opera star, could revoke a license, gratuitously granted, to use her name and portrait in the advertisement of perfumes. The court issued an injunction against the further use of her name and portrait by the perfume company, even though the company had trade-marked its product (using name and portrait of Mary Garden) and had invested considerable amounts of money to popularize them.

In *Lane v. F. W. Woolworth Co.* (1939), the sale of lockets containing the picture of actress Judy Lane was held to be in violation of the statute.

In *Neyland v. Home Patterns Co.* (1933), the court held that the use of a painter's name, without his consent, to promote sales of patterns for reproducing the painter's artistic productions by means of embroidery (the productions not having been sold or disposed of by him), was a violation of the privacy statute.

Now there is a portion of section 51 which says that:

> . . . nothing contained in this act shall be so construed as to prevent any person, firm or corporation from using the name, portrait or picture of any manufacturer or dealer in connection with the goods, wares and merchandise manufactured, produced or dealt in by him which he has sold or disposed of with such name, portrait or picture used in connection therewith; or from using the name, portrait or picture of any author, composer or artist in connection with his literary, musical or artistic productions which he has sold or disposed of with such name, portrait or picture used in connection therewith.

Taken literally, this means that if Adam Adams sells or otherwise disposes of an item which he has produced or handled in business, and has used his name in connection with such item, then any person may use the name of Adam Adams in connection with that item. So that if Adam Adams manufactured a garment, attached a label containing his name, and sold it to a retailer, the retailer could lawfully advertise the garment as one manufactured by Adam Adams. But then a case comes up involving facts which vary from this simple example.

One Jaccard designed a dress. Then someone, having observed the dress, and without Jaccard's consent, decided to print up patterns which could be sold to "do it yourself" consumers. The patterns were placed on sale in a department store, and Jaccard's name was used in the promotion of their sale. Was this a use in violation of the privacy statute? In *Jaccard v. R. H. Macy & Co.* (1942), it was held that the name of a dress designer could lawfully be used in connection with the sale of patterns to be used by consumers in making dresses designed by him. The court said that the exposure of a dress to public view placed it in the public domain, and that, in the absence of unfair competition, anyone had the right to copy it, or sell patterns thereof, and in so doing could truthfully state the name of the designer. The court did not justify its decision on the basis of that portion of section 51 which has been quoted above. And yet, is not that portion the only part of the law that allows the use of a name, without consent, for commercial purposes?

And when *Shostakovich v. Twentieth Century-Fox Film Corp.* came up in 1945, the *Jaccard* case was pointed to as the basis for denying the relief prayed for. Dmitri Shostakovich and three other Russian composers thought they had a cause of action when their names appeared among the "credits" displayed in connection with a motion picture called *The Iron Curtain*. They had not given any consent to the use of their names or their music. No consent was necessary with respect to the music, for it was not protected under the copyright laws. Yet, had such music been "sold or disposed of" as contemplated by the pertinent provision in section 51? Again, the court did not refer to that provision, but based its conclusion solely on the finding in the *Jaccard* case. The court in each case seemed to be applying its own standard of justice rather than applying the letter of the law.

Let us now turn to other categories of cases in which the privacy statute has been interpreted and applied. Most of the complaints that have arisen since passage of the statute have been concerned with the use of names, portraits and pictures in newspapers, magazines, books, and motion pictures. Did the legislature think of these categories? It at least thought of advertising as it might be included in these *media* of communication. But did it think of these *media* in terms of potential uses of names and pictures for trade purposes? The statute followed close upon the heels of the Roberson decision, which had to do with advertising. The fact that the term "trade" was included along with "advertising" made it obvious that the legislature thought of names and pictures being used in connection with ordinary articles of trade. Since the language of the statute was general, neither including nor excluding *media* of communication specifically, it remained for the courts to give the statute meaning in this respect. Why was this such a problem? Because of our interest in a free press. But no freedom is absolute—even that of the press. Libel laws have limited that freedom. Was it to be limited further by the law of privacy?

Newspapers

Jeffries v. New York Journal Publishing Company, decided in 1910, gave an early clue as to how the privacy statute would be applied to cases involving newspapers. Jim Jeffries, formerly the heavyweight boxing champion of the world, had been in the process of writing his autobiography when the *New York Evening Journal* decided to publish a series of articles on the biography of the pugilist, together with illustrations. Viewing the situation from the standpoint of Jeffries and the prospective sales of his work, how would you feel about the anticipatory action on the part of the newspaper people? Needless to say, it angered him, and he sued for an injunction. The relief he sought was denied. The court said:

> In my opinion a picture is not used "for advertising purposes" within its meaning unless the picture is part of an advertisement, while "trade" refers to "commerce or traffic," not to the dissemination of information.

It was thus made clear that the dissemination of information was not to be considered "trade," and that the use of names or pictures in such process would not be deemed a use for trade purposes.

One can hardly think of privacy without contemplating its association with information. Certainly the disclosure of that which is private is an invasion of privacy. The statute, however, did not speak of disclosures. It spoke not only of the use of names, pictures and portraits, but it also spoke of purposes—and cannot information be disseminated for commercial purposes? When the name, picture or portrait of an individual is included in such information, can it not be said that such inclusion was a use for commercial purposes? Shall we say that the dissemination of information is so important that we must not stop to inquire into motives? What is so earthshaking about the biography of a boxer that the use of his name and pictures, in that connection, should be categorically considered as lying beyond the purposes of trade?

Suppose it is conceded that the public has an interest in the lives of public figures, and that biographies of such persons are considered informative rather than commercial. Can the publication of forgotten facts concerning a private individual be given the same classification?

How would you feel about the woman confronted by the situation revealed in the following case? In 1905, a man went through a marriage ceremony and then disappeared. The report of his disappearance drew attention to the fact that he had been previously married to a woman whose death had caused at least a spark of suspicion. The spark was revived. The body was exhumed. It was found that the death had been caused by poisoning. The search for this suspected murderer led to a rooming house in New York, and he was captured as he was moving in two new trunks. He was being aided by the landlady, whom he had been courting. Conviction and execution followed, as did the newspaper story. Naturally, the account included that portion of the happenings in which the landlady had played a minor role. She did not complain. However, when the same story reappeared in the same newspaper more than twenty-five years later, the landlady, now much older and more sensitive to affronts upon her dignity, found her former wound reborn. This time she complained.

What purpose was meant to be served by the republication? Granted that there was a purpose, were the feelings of this woman considered? She was convinced that she had been legally wronged, but the court could not bring itself to agree with her. Few would find comfort in the explanation given by the court in these words:

> Except to the limited extent provided by statute (section 50), there is no right of privacy . . . Written words, the effect of which is to invade privacy and to bring undesired notoriety, are without remedy, unless they also appreciably affect reputation. This is the domain, not of positive law, but of obedience to the unenforceable . . . From such harms one is protected only by the code of common decency. (*Kimmerle v. New York Evening Journal*).

It may be concluded that newspapers cannot be held in violation of the privacy statute for reporting any facts, past or present, concerning public or private personages. Of course, newspapers can be held liable for insertions of names and pictures in advertisements. But what if a news item appears within advertising space?

In *Wallach v. Bacharach* (1948), the plaintiff's name appeared in a news item which was included in space devoted to the advertisement of a product. There was no connection between the news item and the advertisement, but there they stood side by side in a box. Why was this done? There could be no question but that it was done to attract the attention of readers to the advertisement. The court felt that, since there was no relationship between the news report and the product advertised, it could not be said that this was a use of plaintiff's name for advertising or trade purposes. In a broad sense, one could not escape the conclusion that this was a use for advertising purposes. However, the court backed up its own conclusion by quoting authority:

> It is well established that every incidental mention of some person's name in connection with advertising or trade does not constitute a violation of the provisions under consideration.

And so it may also be concluded that, to constitute a ground for liability, the violation of the statutory provisions must be more than technical—it must be substantial.

Magazines

The newspaper cases have told us that the use of names and pictures in the dissemination of information is not to be considered a use for trade purposes. The magazine cases will indicate that this is not a hard and fast rule. We shall see a distinction drawn between dissemination of information for the purpose of enlightenment and dissemination of information for the purpose of amusement. According to this distinction, complaints falling on one side of the line must fail, while those falling on the other side of the line deserve to succeed. As we examine the decisions, it will become obvious that the distinction is more easily stated than applied.

The first case in which the distinction might have been applied was *Colyer v. Richard K. Fox Pub. Co.* (1914). However, the plaintiff followed another line of attack, and the court decided the case on that basis.

Plaintiff was a professional high diver. A picture of her, attired in her professional costume, revealing and appealing, was placed on a page of the *National Police Gazette* together with the pictures of four other female vaudevillians in their customary costumes. Beneath the picture were the following words: "Five of a kind on this page. Most of them adorn the burlesque stage; all of them are favorites with the bald-headed boys." The plaintiff claimed that her picture had been used for advertising purposes in violation of the statute. The court thought otherwise, and its decision was affirmed by the Appellate Division. The upper court described the periodical in this way: "It carries a very considerable amount of reading matter that scarcely appeals to a refined mind, and likewise a great number of advertisements of quack nostrums and trivial things." In other words, this was not a magazine designed to disseminate information of public import, but rather one that combined entertainment with advertisement. What the plaintiff had in mind was that the primary aim of the magazine was advertisement, and that the non-advertising materials were designed to attract attention and thereby bring prospective consumers in contact with the advertisements. She, therefore, contended that advertising was the purpose for which her picture had been included.

The plaintiff's argument seemed plausible, but the court would not go along:

> Applied as the appellant would desire, it would cover every issue of our newspapers, and especially our great number of monthly magazines, in which the advertising matter is as great in bulk and oftentimes as interesting, as the letterpress.

It was also the opinion of the court that the statute was not aimed at eliminating the portrayal of persons who had distinguished themselves in their occupations.

Here we have the first hint of an attitude that, in applying the provisions of the privacy statute, the treatment accorded to cases involving distinguished personalities should be different from that given to cases involving unknowns. Judge Parker, in the *Roberson* case, had frowned upon any judicial attempt to draw such a distinction, suggesting that, if any distinction of that sort was deemed desirable, the legislature was the proper body to promulgate it. A re-reading of sections 50 and 51 would reveal that this was not done.

Moving chronologically through the magazine cases, we come to *Martin v. New Metropolitan Fiction* (1931). Plaintiff was the mother of a girl who had met her fate at the hands of her slayer. Defendant was the publisher of *True Detective Mysteries*. One of the issues of that magazine contained a story entitled "Tropic Vengeance." It dealt with the murder itself and the trial of the alleged culprit. A courtroom scene was pictorially included, beneath which were these words: "As Lozade passed close by, on his way to the witness stand, the broken-hearted mother cried out: 'I could kill that man with my own hands'!" Plaintiff contended that the picture had been used for commercial purposes. The trial judge reviewed the cases involving claims of invasion by the use of pictures, then spoke as follows:

> Apparently legitimate use of names and pictures in commercial enterprises depends upon the purpose, viewing the matter from the standpoint of the reaction of the public rather than from the standpoint of the person

who uses them. Names and pictures are legitimately used in connection with mere items of news, with matters of history of public men and events, and with matters which are submitted to the public in a way which invites public comment. Even private social affairs and prevailing fashions involving individuals who make no bid for publicity are, by custom, regarded as public property, where the apparent use is to convey information of interest and not mere advertising.

The use of names and pictures, in the various ways mentioned, are generally important features in many commerical ventures and their success aided thereby. Nevertheless, from the standpoint of the public, the use is not for purposes of trade. The distinction is well illustrated by the motion picture cases. Such pictures portraying current events are regarded by the public as primarily educational rather than commercial, while a mere dramatization of the same events would be considered essentially commercial.

The court went on to say that perpetrators of crime brought themselves into the public domain, as did also those employed in the detection of crime and those occupying public places. To a certain extent, victims were also included. As for third parties, said the court:

Third parties may in some instances become so involved by mere accident that it would be impossible to omit the part they play in a fair and intelligent chronicle of the events.

The court found no such involvement on the part of the mother in this case, saying:

From the standpoint of the reader of the magazine, the conclusion would be, ordinarily, that the picture of plaintiff with its accompanying lurid and passionate quotation attributed to her was inserted simply to add to the attractiveness and sale of the publication. Such a use I do not believe to be legitimate, but rather a commerical one.

The trial court decided in favor of the plaintiff. On appeal, the Appellate Division first affirmed the decision and then reversed it, without an explanatory opinion.

Had the trial court's decision been upheld, it would have been possible to say that, with respect to materials appearing in magazines, a distinction had been established between uses for the purpose of informing and uses for the purpose of attracting trade. While it seemed inevitable that an aggrieved party would eventually prevail on the basis of such distinction, the courts moved in that direction at a painfully sluggish pace.

The *Sarat Lahiri v. Daily Mirror* (1937) case arose as the result of a pictorial illustration included in an article appearing in the magazine section of a Sunday newspaper. The article was entitled "I Saw

The Famous Rope Trick (But It Didn't Really Happen)." It had been inspired by the offer of a large sum of money, by a British society of mystics, to anyone who could cause a coil of rope to rise unaided until one end be suspended in mid-air, against the force of gravity. This was known as the Hindu "Rope Trick." The author of the article attempted to show that this trick was done through the exercise of hypnotic powers and the creation of an illusion, and that the ability to create such illusions had been achieved through the cultivation of an occult philosophy developed long ago in the Far East. Photographic illustrations were used. One consisted of a series of specially posed colored photographs of a humorous nature, portraying the rising of a rope and its ascension by a woman. And toward the end of the article there were three pictures: the first, "India's Holy Men Studying;" the second, the tower where the trick had been performed; and the third, a reproduction of a professional photograph showing Sarat Lahiri, well known Hindu musician, playing a musical instrument as accompaniment to an Indian female dancer. Feeling that his photograph had been used for trade purposes, Lahiri brought action. His claim was denied.

The court reasoned that the article concerned matters having a legitimate news interest; that plaintiff's photograph had a relationship to the article; and that the photograph was used to illustrate the points which the author had the desire to demonstrate. In what way did Lahiri's picture enhance the informative purpose of the article? Was it really inserted to put across a point? The court thought so:

> There could have been no other motive for putting it in. It would be far-fetched to hold in this case that the picture was not used in an illustrative sense, but merely to promote the sale of the paper.

Miss Colyer, Mrs. Martin, and Mr. Lahiri all failed to convince the judiciary that their likenesses had been used for the purposes of trade. Were their views so far-fetched? Was the guarantee of a free press meant to explode all caves of privacy?

History tells us of despotic rulers who could not bear the thrusts of criticism and who punished with severity their rhetorical and literary tormenters. It was to eliminate the possibility of attempts to suppress criticism of the Government and its administration that guarantees of free speech and free press were found to be necessary and proper. Can it possibly be said that those who formulated these guarantees had in mind to encourage gossip and to insure the legality of freely capitalizing upon individual personality? Was not the guarantee

meant to insure enlightenment rather than exploitation? Was it meant
to encompass the satisfaction of idle curiosity as an area within which
freedom of the press might be exercised without restraint? Assuming
the answer to be no, why should the courts be so conservative in applying the prohibitions of the New York privacy statute?

We move on to 1940 and the case of *Sidis v. F-R Pub. Co.* Back in
1910, William James Sidis was a child prodigy. At the age of eleven,
he lectured to distinguished mathematicians on the subject of Four-
Dimensional Bodies. He graduated from Harvard College at the age
of sixteen. From the eruption of his genius until his college gradua-
tion, newspaper readers were well acquainted with his prowess. Then
he disappeared from public view, and only occasionally was reference
made to him in the press. He withdrew from his life of fame and
chose a life of privacy.

Suddenly, in August, 1937, the shell of privacy into which Sidis had
recoiled was caused to explode by the publication of a biographical
sketch in *The New Yorker,* a weekly magazine. The forthcoming
sketch had been announced in a newspaper advertisement. It appeared
in a section devoted to sketches of present and past personalities, under
the title, "Where Are They Now?", and the subtitle, "April Fool."
The subtitle was explained at the end of the article by a statement,
made by Sidis in an interview, to the effect that he had been born on
April Fool's Day.

After covering Sidis' early years, the article went on to reveal his
breakdown and his ensuing revulsion for his former life of fame and
scholarship. The former mathematical genius was pictured as an
eccentric who persisted in attempting to hide his identity, who chose
the career of an insignificant clerk requiring little mathematical talent, who collected streetcar transfers with enthusiasm, who acquired
a deep interest in the lore of the Okamakammessett Indians, whose
lodging consisted of an untidy hall bedroom in Boston's shabby south
end, whose laugh was curious, whose manner of speech was peculiar,
and whose other personal habits bore out his misfortune.

Sidis had neither sought nor consented to the exposure of his current way of life. He felt, therefore, that the publication was an unwarranted intrusion upon his privacy. He found no relief in the
courts. Once again the New York privacy statute was called into play.
And again the outcome of a case depended on whether or not a portrayal had been used for the purposes of trade. One would have been
tempted to bet on Sidis after reading the following portion of the
opinion:

It is not contended that any of the matter printed is untrue. Nor is the manner of the author unfriendly; Sidis today is described as having "a certain childlike charm." But the article is merciless in its dissection of intimate details of its subject's personal life, and this in company with elaborate accounts of Sidis' passion for privacy and the pitiable lengths to which he has gone in order to avoid public scrutiny. The work possesses great reader interest, for it is both amusing and instructive; but it may be fairly described as a ruthless exposure of a once public character, who has since sought and has now been deprived of the seclusion of private life.

One can feel in the description given by the court the misery experienced by Sidis at the hands of those responsible for the exposure of his privacy. Was this exposure justified? What purpose did it serve? Whose interest did it promote? The court said that the work was both amusing and instructive. To the extent of supplying information it may be said to have been instructive, but is all impartation of information instructive in the sense of being educational? The purpose of education is not the mere satisfaction of idle curiosity, but rather to stimulate the mind to the end that it may grapple with human problems and lead toward the fulfillment of human aspirations. The exposure of private affairs can hardly be considered the product of a purpose to stimulate achievement.

It was not until 1950 that the sun began to shine upon those whose privacy was being invaded in magazines. The sun shone, however, through broken clouds which made the outcomes of future cases unpredictable. In *Sutton v. Hearst Corp.,* the court held that the portrayal of a person in a magazine story could be found to have been a use for trade purposes, and that the facts of the case indicated such possibility. What were the facts?

The story appeared in the magazine section of a Sunday newspaper. It was heralded by the words: "Here, told for the first time in all its poignant and dramatic detail, is one of the great true love stories of our time. . . . A Flower a Week Forever for a Girl He Could Not Have . . . with a surprise ending." The story was discovered as the result of court proceedings concerned with the will of a turret gunner who had been shot down during World War II over Linz, Germany. The gunner had known the plaintiff before he went into the service, for they had worked in the same office. The article went on to tell about plaintiff's engagement and marriage to another man, and about the birth of their first child. There was nothing startling about all this, for there had never been anything between plaintiff and the turret gun-

ner, and she had forgotten about him. The startling part came with
the revelation that he had not forgotten her. His will contained a provision by the terms of which a sum of money was to be administered
by his brother for the purpose of providing the plaintiff, the girl of
his dreams, with one perfect rose each week for the remainder of her
life. The article contained a sketch of a woman cupping in her hands
the "one perfect rose."

So here was a happily married woman, about to give birth to her
second child, who was confronted with this embarrassing publicity.
It would seem doubtful that the revelation through a straight news
item could have been attacked. But the manner in which her involvement was reported, a dramatically presented magazine story, gave rise
to the question of purpose. The defendant contended that plaintiff
had failed to make out a case and moved that the complaint be dismissed, but the court denied the motion. The Appellate Division
upheld this decision by a vote of three-to-two. According to the majority, the plaintiff had stated a case, and there remained for determination only the question as to the purpose of the magazine story. This
was a question to be decided by a jury. The matter was aptly explained
in this way:

> It is for the triers of the facts to determine whether the article and its
> surrounding illustrations were limited to reporting fairly past or current
> events, whether it is educational or informative, or whether the primary
> purpose, as the complaint alleges, was to amuse and astonish the reading
> public, not for the legitimate purpose of disseminating news, but for
> "purposes of trade;" viz., the publisher's profits through increased cir-
> culation induced by such exploitation of plaintiff without her consent
> and against her will.

Thus, at last, the application of the privacy statute to the contents
of magazines was established. It was finally recognized that a distinction
could be drawn between uses of magazine material for "the legitimate
purpose of disseminating news" and for "the purposes of trade." The
distinction lay between the purpose to inform and the purpose to
amuse; between the purpose to enlighten and the purpose to promote
sales. Yet, this distinction has not, since its inception, been applied
with consistency.

In *Oma v. Hillman Periodicals* (1953), the court conceded that
Oma's picture had been placed on the back cover of a magazine for
the purpose of promoting the sale of that publication, but refused to
grant relief. The case was decided by a three-to-two vote. What were
the facts?

Oma's picture appeared on the back cover of a magazine with the caption: "Tycoon—this man can make $25,000 on a single deal, but it might cost him his life. Why? See page 24." Oma was a well-known boxer. An article about boxing began on page 24. Was the article about Oma? No. Did it mention Oma? No. The only connection between Oma and the article was that he was a boxer, and the article was about boxing. The court felt that the picture was a relevant illustration of an article on a matter of public interest, and that it was "immaterial that its manner of use and placement was designed to sell the article so that it might be paid for and read."

The dissenting opinion took this view:

> The use of plaintiff's name and photograph on the back cover of defendant's magazine does not, in my opinion, fall into the category of any exemption defined by previous decisions under the Civil Rights Law. The inside of the article referred to on the outside cover was not about plaintiff as a public figure. He was in no way mentioned in the article or referred to in any way. Nor was he even used as an illustration. The photograph, its pose, and place on the cover were plainly used to catch the eye and advertise the magazine and the article. I think that is not a permissible use of one's name and visage and that plaintiff is not subject to such use because he happened to be a public figure in a sense.

Perhaps the majority was influenced by the fact that Oma was a public figure. However, the privacy statute did not differentiate between public and private figures. And yet, the courts have seemed to be more willing to detect commercial purposes in the portrayal of private individuals than in the portrayal of well-known personalities. Public interest in a matter under discussion should not be allowed to justify clear exploitations of personality, public or private. A step in that direction was taken in the case of *Metzger v. Dell Pub. Co.* (1955).

The case involved a magazine story, "Gang Boy," published in *Front Page Detective*. A free lance reporter was inspired to write the story following the arrest of a young man who was charged with beating up two men. In order to give his story authenticity, the author spent two weeks in the vicinity of the crime, seeking to unearth the reasons behind the facts. The court gave its appraisal of the story:

> A fair summary of what the article sets forth as the reporter's conclusions from what he saw and heard is that in a more or less generally described section of Brooklyn youths who have little to do in their spare time have a habit of standing around on the streets, looking longingly through tavern windows at the light, warmth, entertainment, and companionship to be seen therein, and of playing cards or throwing dice in hallways, and

having organized themselves into lawless gangs, and in that way get caught in the meshes of the law.

While not a news report; the article thus fairly may be said to be an attempt to portray the existence of a condition which indisputably is a subject of legitimate public interest. Somewhat differently phrased, the article may be described as a survey of a social condition.

Where did the article go wrong? The three plaintiffs, who were minors, happened to be around when the reporter was in the neighborhood looking for "local color," and he took their pictures and included them within the confines of the story. This, felt the court, was going too far:

> ... and I think it difficult to conceive of a more flagrant violation of that right than is here presented; and if the statute does not cover such a case as this it might just as well be repealed as a wholly ineffectual means of protecting the right it is supposed to create and recognize. The fact that it is legitimate to discuss the existence of gangs and gangsters does not make it legitimate to drag these plaintiffs into the discussion.

No definite conclusions can be drawn from the line of cases involving the use of names and portrayals in magazines. While the courts have professed a determination to delineate the respective areas of permissible and prohibited uses, the results have not indicated complete success. A line of demarcation has been drawn between the purpose to inform and the aim to amuse, but its course seems to lie somewhat wide of the legislative mark.

Books

Books fall roughly into two classifications, fiction and non-fiction. Fictional works are generally considered to involve trade purposes, while non-fictional works are generally considered to be aimed at the dissemination of information. It therefore follows that uses of names and portrayals in fictional works are to be treated as violations of the privacy statute, while similar uses in non-fictional works are to be treated as permissible. However, no matter how clear and simple the statement of a principle may sound, difficulties are bound to arise in attempting to apply its meaning to particular cases as they arise.

The case of *Ellis v. Hurst* (1910) presented a peculiar problem. Edward S. Ellis was an outstanding writer of juvenile and historical works. He wrote under the pen name of Lieutenant R. H. Jayne. A book publisher named Hurst, having found two books which had been written and published by Ellis without copyright protection, decided to republish them under the pen name (which he had a right to do). What Ellis complained of, however, was the use of his real name on the covers and wrappers of the books. Was this necessary or propitious? Did this use aid a purpose to inform? Did it not strike at the very heart of privacy? The injunction sought by Ellis was denied, the court being of the opinion that the right to publish uncopyrighted books, published under a nom de plume, carried with it the right to state the true name of the author.

With regard to fictional works, usually in the form of novels, the greatest problem has been the matter of identifying actual persons with characters portrayed. In the one case in which the identification was readily apparent, the court held that only one mention of a person in a work was insignificant. (Damron v. Doubleday, Doran & Co. (1928). In other cases the identifications were considered insufficient.

Swacker v. Wright (1935) involved the use of plaintiff's name in a book called *The Benson Murder Case*. Frank M. Swacker was an attorney who, in the course of his career, had acted as special assistant to the Attorney General of the United States in the prosecution of antitrust cases. The name "Frank Swacker" was used in the book to depict the secretary to the district attorney and was included, in that form, only in the cast of characters. The surname "Swacker" alone was used in the text. The court said: "The mere use of the plaintiff's surname and Christian name with his middle initial omitted without any other identifying feature cannot be held a suffcent basis for relief under the statute."

People v. Charles Scribner's Sons (1954) presented a similar situation. Joseph Anthony Maggio had been a member of the same military company in Hawaii as James Jones, author of *From Here to Eternity*. One of the characters in the book was called "Angelo Maggio." The book did not place "Maggio" in Company F, Maggio's company, nor did it portray any acts performed by the complainant. His claim of invasion was based solely on the identity of the surnames and his connection with the author. The court realized that Jones may have had his former companymate in mind when he created "Maggio," but discounted the significance of that possibility: "So long as the author does not use the true name of the character he may have had in mind, there is no basis for complaint."

It may be seen from the two foregoing cases that, where the element of identification is questionable, the true full name of a person must be used before a violation of the privacy statute, through fictional works, will be recognized. However, cannot persons be portrayed in works of fiction without their true names being used? Cannot portraits be made by verbal expression as well as by the strokes of a brush or the clicking of a camera? Suppose a novelist portrays an episode in the life of a person because it makes a good story and will sell. He dresses it up for dramatic effect. He knows that if he uses the true name of his chief character he will face liability under the privacy statute. So he gives the character another name and makes other fictitious changes to suit his purpose. Surely the law has proved itself capable of piercing veils and disguises. Is it willing to do the same in privacy cases?

Toscani v. Hershey (1946) arose from the complaint of one who had found himself and his activities fictionally portrayed in a novel and play entitled *A Bell for Adano*. The central figure in those works was a person fictitiously called "Major Vicor Joppolo." He was described as the senior civil affairs officer of the Allied Military Government in a Sicilian town fictitiously called "Adano." Plaintiff alleged that the events and acts narrated in the novel and play related to him, and that he had been, in fact, the senior officer of the Allied Military Government in the town of Licata, Sicily, during the occupation of that town by the Allied Armies in World War II.

Assuming the truth of the allegations, and further assuming that fictional portrayals of actual persons were to be considered uses for trade purposes, a result favorable to the plaintiff seemed inevitable. However, the court did not feel so inclined, as it said:

> Giving to the language used in section 51 its ordinary meaning, we find that it was not intended to give a living person a cause of action based on the mere portrayal of acts and events concerning a person designated fictitiously in a novel or play merely because the actual experiences of the living person had been similar to the acts and events so narrated.

A dissenting judge called attention to a distinction between basing a novel or play on events that occurred during the life of a living person and the fictional portrayal, for trade purposes, of a living person as the chief character in a play.

It may be seen, from the foregoing illustrations, that fictional portrayals in novels afford virtually no basis for recovery under the New York privacy statute. When a person succeeds in identifying himself with a fictional character and still loses the case, judicial interpretation of the statutory prohibition is indeed very narrow.

If courts failed to recognize violations of the statute in cases involving fictional works, what hope was there that favorable results would be obtained in cases concerned with nonfictional works? Certainly these would be justified on the basis of public interest. It would have to be conceded that the use of names and portrayals in nonfictional works would be beyond attack if such use furthered an aim to be informative regarding matters of current interest. The cases of *People v. McBride* (1936) and *Kline v. McBride* (1939), involving the book called *I Break Strikes,* were decided on that basis. But how should a biography, concerning no topic of current interest, be treated?

Koussevitzky v. Allen, Towne & Heath (1944) dealt with the biography of Serge Koussevitzky, most distinguished conductor of the world-renowned Boston Symphony Orchestra. While still alive, and having refused authorization, he became the subject of a biography published by the defendant. The book contained pictures, used without his consent, and was dressed in the usual jacket designed to attract attention. Not only was this eminent figure displeased with such unauthorized exposure of his life's story, but, meticulous and exacting as he was in his musicianship, he was apprehensive and disturbed regarding inaccuracies discovered in the publication. He took offense to what he considered a brazen transgression and sought an injunction against further distribution of the book. He soon learned that the statute entitled "Right of Privacy" would afford him no protection against the invasion that had left him sorely perplexed. The court said:

> The right of privacy statute does not apply to an unauthorized biography of a public figure unless the biography is fictional or novelized in character. An examination of the book complained of clearly shows that it is not fictional. That it may contain untrue statements does not transform it into the class of fiction.

There is a new type of book that has come upon the scene in recent years—the comic book. What is its purpose? Do people read it for the purpose of enlightenment? Are its publishers bent on being informative? Shall the use of names and portrayals within its covers be considered uses for trade purposes? These questions confronted the court in *Molony v. Boy Comics Publishers* (1950).

On July 28, 1945, a United States Army bomber crashed into the Empire State Building in New York City. It struck at the seventy-ninth floor, and all occupants of the plane were killed. Aside from the initial crash, the explosions and flames that followed severely burned and maimed many people working on or in the vicinity of the seventy-ninth floor. One elevator fell from that height to the ground floor and all the other elevators were temporarily put out of commission.

Donald P. Molony became a hero when he outdid himself in hurriedly procuring medical supplies, giving first aid, climbing endless stairs, and carrying out survivors. His heroism, along with all other details of the catastrophe, was reported in all the papers. It excited the nation, for here in a small way was a tiny sample of possible disaster that could result from attacks by enemy bombers. This was news, and the press did a good job in disseminating it. It was what happened afterwards that gave Molony reason to complain.

Six months after the incident the heroism of Donald Molony was reiterated, when an account of the story was related through five pages of comic strips published in *Boy Comics*. Molony brought action under section 51 of the Civil Rights Law, claiming that the pictorial account of his heroism was a use of his name and portrait for trade purposes. His success in the lower court was short-lived, for the judgment of that court was reversed on appeal by a vote of three-to-two. Said the majority:

> We think that this article is not to be classed as fictional merely for the reason that it is presented pictorially, by a schematic representation of the events depicted in the form of rough sketches which do not purport to be exact replicas of the original subjects. Comic strips are, to some extent, a throwback to the origin of language, typified by the word "hieroglyph," which refers primarily to the picture-writing of the ancient Egyptians, or the figure-writing of the Chinese, Aztecs, and ancient Peruvians .If such form of expression appeals to immaturity, it may hark back to the childhood of civilization, but one may think that it is nonetheless a medium of expression akin to language, and capably of being employed for the same varied uses. It does not follow that plaintiff's exploit has been fictionalized merely for the reason that it has been told through a form of picture-writing, which is as old as the human race.

Let us remember that the legislature did not distinguish between uses in fictional works and uses in nonfictional works. The legislature spoke only of purpose. It was not necessary, therefore, to classify Molony's portrayal as fictional in order to find that it had been used for trade purposes. The court seemed so entranced by its expedition into the origin of comic strips, that it appeared to overlook the element of purpose. The dissenters were not so entranced:

> However, if the design of the writer is to amuse the readers and with that object in mind, he magnifies and exaggerates the story so as to produce greater revenue, the immunity is lost. Where the prime motive of the publication is amusement for trade purposes, as a matter of law, the purpose is commerical.

We have gone far enough to see that the courts in general have an aversion to declaring any publication of any sort a violation of the privacy statute.

Motion Pictures

The motion picture cases give further evidence of judicial restraint in applying the provisions of the privacy statute. While this category provides two cases in which the legislative intent seems to have been perfectly applied, it also presents two other cases in which the results are questionable. The tests are the same as those applied to other media of communication, and the outcomes are equally unpredictable, except that a bet on the defendant has already been shown to be pretty safe. As an experiment, let us keep in mind *Molony v. Boy Comics,* reported above, as we consider *Binns v. Vitagraph Co. of America* (1913).

On January 23, 1909, the steamships Republic and Florida collided at sea. The Republic was equipped with machines for sending and receiving messages by wireless telegraphy. Binns, an operator of one of such machines, was the first man to use wireless telegraphy at a time when its use resulted in the saving of hundreds of lives. He was, therefore, somewhat of a hero. As one could imagine, the newspapers carried full accounts of the event.

At this time, the Vitagraph Company was in the business of producing, leasing, selling, and displaying motion pictures. After reading the newspaper accounts of the incident, the agents of the company made a series of films depicting the event and including, of course, the heroic role played by Binns. The films were shown in many places. Binns, feeling aggrieved, brought action under the Civil Rights Law and won a judgment. The court found that the portrayal of Binns had been used for trade purposes. It was felt that, if amusement of the public was the object, the portrayal of a person should be considered a use for trade purposes; and conversely, if education of the public was the object, the conduct of a party in portraying another should be regarded as falling beyond the statutory proscription.

Why was this case not followed in *Molony v. Boy Comics?* Was there a distinction between the basic facts of the respective cases? Could it be that in 1913 motion pictures were generally considered commercial in nature, while other forms of communication were considered primarily aimed at the dissemination of information? By 1919, the dual purpose of motion pictures was established in *Humiston v. Universal Film Mfg. Co.,* wherein it was held that portrayal of a person in a newsreel was not a violation of the privacy statute. Should a comic book be classed as a medium aimed at the dissemination of information, or should it not rather be classed as a device aimed at amusement?

While the reasoning of *Binns* was overlooked in *Molony,* the *Metzger* case (reported above), relating to the portrayal of innocent bystanders for "local color" in a magazine article, did follow the reasoning in another motion picture case.

Blumenthal v. Picture Classics (1932) lent encouragement to those who believed in the inviolate personality. The defendant was a motion picture company that had decided to make a travelogue depicting life in the various sections of New York City. To that end, two actors were chosen to be filmed touring the city and commenting on what they saw. The picture was entitled *Sight-Seeing in New York City with Nick and Tony.* It included a scene in which the plaintiff, a widow, was shown as she was engaged in selling bread and rolls to passersby on Orchard Street. There is no need to describe the feelings of this woman who, because of her widowhood, was so engaged in order to earn a livelihood. It would be easy for others to say that she did nothing of which she should feel ashamed, and yet she was entitled to protection from whatever unfavorable views others might take. The court could have said that her portrayal was factual, and that it was relevant to the communication of matters in which the public had an interest. But the court found that the portrayal was aimed at adding color to the production. And the court in the *Metzger* case detected the same design.

Let us keep the *Blumenthal* case in mind as we consider the case of *Sweenck v. Pathe News* (1936).

The plaintiff was a woman who had enrolled in a course of exercises offered gratuitously by the proprietor of a gymnasium. The course was open to all females who weighed more than two hundred pounds. Without obtaining consent as required by the privacy statute, the defendant took pictures of the women while they were exercising and displayed them in theaters. The camera, of course, had included the plaintiff within its focus. In many instances, the women were using a new and unique apparatus which aided them in their exercises.

Realizing the not always welcome impression sometimes conveyed, to the mental eyes of others, by the portrayal of one's God-given physique in gymnasium attire, could this woman be blamed for the feeling that her privacy had been invaded? Should it be said to her that this exposure was justified by the public interest in a demonstration of some novel and unique apparatus? Would she not answer that other methods of producing the same instructional effect were available? She felt entitled to redress, and so she informed the court, but to no avail.

The court held that matters of public interest appearing in newspapers and newsreels were not in violation of the privacy statute. Said the court:

> While it may be difficult in some instances to find the point at which public interest ends, it seems reasonably clear that pictures of a group of corpulent women attempting to reduce with the aid of some rather novel and unique apparatus do not cross the borderline, at least so long as a large proportion of the female sex continues its present concern about any increase in poundage. The amusing comments which accompanied the pictures did not detract from their news value.

Was there really a difference between the *Blumenthal* case and the *Sweenck* case? If public interest was a factor, was it not greater in the former than in the latter? Surely the public would have a deeper interest in the make-up of a community than in methods used for the reduction of weight. Was not the portrayal of overweight women meant for amusement, as the portrayal of a street-vendor was meant for color?

While the treatment of factual portrayals seems to have been inconsistent, the scrutiny applied to fictional works seems to follow a pattern of unbroken consistency. Whereas fictional portrayals are considered uses for trade purposes, plaintiffs continue to encounter difficulty in attempts to identify themselves with fictitious characters. We have seen the difficulty experienced in the book cases. Let us view it now as it appears in a motion picture case.

Levey v. Warner Bros. (1944) arose as the result of a film called *Yankee Doodle Dandy*. The action was brought by Ethel Levey, one-time wife of the late George M. Cohan, whose life was fictionally portrayed in the picture. Her complaint was not based upon Cohan's portrayal, but rather upon her own. The outcome of the case depended upon a comparison of her role in the life of the central figure with the role of a fictitious character called "Mary." Ethel claimed that she was portrayed in the picture through "Mary."

It seems that in 1898, at the age of seventeen, Ethel had already established herself as an actress and singer on the vaudeville stage, when she was invited to a gathering in a Chicago hotel room. Cohan was there. They met. He was then about twenty and had been performing with his mother, father, and sister. It was love at first sight, for his proposal of marriage came at their very first meeting. He immediately gave her two songs, which she sang at an "opening" a short time later, and continued to compose songs for his sweetheart to sing at her later performances. They were married during the following year and, thereafter, she took leading parts in shows he wrote and produced. It was largely through her efforts that Sam Harris was induced, in 1904, to finance *Little Johnny Jones,* an outstanding Cohan success. In 1905, when Cohan's *Forty-Five Minutes From Broadway* opened in Chicago, she sat in a box with him and his parents, while on stage, Fay Templeton sang *"Mary."* They were separated in 1906 and divorced in 1907. He remarried the same year and lived with his second wife until his death in 1942. This was Ethel's story, and now for the show.

The court observed certain differences between Ethel's story and the role of "Mary." At the age of seventeen, "Mary," a stage-struck but ambitious girl, after watching Cohan perform, wandered uninvited into his dressing room. He was still wearing the disguise of an old man. They danced for each other. Then Cohan removed the disguise and revealed himself to be a man of about twenty. He immediately became interested in her and began writing songs for her. They met Sam Harris and were successful in obtaining from him financial aid for the production of *Little Johnny Jones,* but not, according to the court, in the manner described by Ethel. "Mary" was later shown in a box with Cohan and Harris at the first performance of *Forty-Five Minutes From Broadway* in New York sometime in 1905. She was wearing a wedding ring. On stage, Fay Templeton was impersonated by Irene Manning, singing "Mary."

Place the two stories side by side and see whether or not there is enough similarity between them to identify "Mary" with Ethel. Of course, a fictional portrayal must by its very nature be different, in some respects, from reality. If such differences are to result in conclusions that a complainant has failed in the essential of identification, how is the classification of fictional portrayals as uses for trade purposes to have any meaning?

The court felt that, whatever similarities there may have been between the events in Ethel's life and episodes in the picture, they were too insignificant to characterize her and were merely incidental to the theme. It was further felt that, even though persons who had known her, or seen her act in the plays from which scenes in the picture had been taken, might be reminded of her participating in them, no one, including herself, could reasonably be led to believe that the actress taking the part of "Mary" was portraying Ethel. The court concluded:

The reproduction in the picture of songs plaintiff sang and scenes in which she took part and the introduction of fictional characters and a largely fictional treatment of Cohan's life may hurt plaintiff's feelings but they do not violate her right of privacy.

All we can say at this point is that cases which fall somewhere in the vicinity of the border line seem to result in decisions favorable to defendants, and even in cases which seem to cross it, the line of demarcation is allowed to shift its position.

Television

Television is the newest and most potent medium of communication. Its beneficial effects may be offset by its abuses. It may be used to disseminate information concerning matters of public interest, provide entertainment, and serve as an advertising agency. In carrying on its functions, it is capable of violating the privacy statute. Knowing the conservative attitude displayed by judges in cases involving other media of communication, we can depend on their finding new reasons for denying relief.

While the statute speaks of purposes as related to the alleged violator, the courts have begun to inquire into the motives of complainants. Why has the suit been brought? Have the feelings of the plaintiff been affected by the invasion of his privacy, or has his suit been prompted by his interest in monetary gain?

It does seem, at times, that complainants are more interested in recovering a share of the receipts of a venture than in enforcing their rights of privacy. This should not affect the outcome of a case if it is demonstrated that, according to the statute, there has been an invasion. If exploitation lies at the heart of invasion, what better method could there be for assessing damages than to accord the victim a share of the profits? And if the statute is to be applied strictly, why should it not be applied as strictly in favor of the plaintiff as it seems to have been applied in favor of the defendant?

The case of *Gautier v. Pro-Football, Inc.* (1952), gives us a relatively recent discussion of the New York line of demarcation as it has been applied to the latest medium of communication, i.e., television. The case presents current judicial thinking with respect to a statute passed fifty years before, at a time when there was no television, not even radio. Television has provided a vast new area of activity with countless opportunities in many directions. The only question with which we are here concerned is how far the operators of this medium may go in portraying persons and events without crossing the statutory line of demarcation.

Gautier was a well-known showman and performer. When hired to do so, he would trot out his ponies, dogs and monkeys (all well-trained animals) and put on his act. He was hired by Pro-Football, Inc., owner of the Washington Redskins, to perform his act between the halves of a football game between the Redskins and the New York Giants to be played in Washington. No thought of television entered the minds of the parties, and the written contract contained no agreement on that score, except that the standard form that was used contained a provision to the effect that no artist would be requested to appear on television without the written consent of the American Guild of Variety Artists.

At this time, the American Broadcasting Company was under contract with the New York Giants to televise home games, and it was agreed that the New York team would try its best to obtain permission for ABC to televise out-of-town games. Such permission was obtained with respect to the game in Washington, where Gautier was scheduled to perform. The ABC announcer chatted with Gautier before the game and informed him that his act was to be televised. Gautier objected but, despite the objection, his act was televised. And the usual commercials were injected both prior to and following the act.

Gautier brought action against Pro-Football, Inc., as well as all others involved in the alleged violation of his rights, including ABC, the advertising agency that had arranged the telecast, and the commercial sponsor. The City Court of the City of New York upheld his claim. The judgment of that court was affirmed by the Appellate Term of the Supreme Court by a vote of three-to-nothing. The Appellate Division reversed the judgment by a vote of four-to-one, and the Court of Appeals agreed with the Appellate Division by a vote of five-to-two. So Gautier passed two hurdles successfully, but was cut down at the higher levels.

Since the opinion handed down by the Appellate Division was lengthier and more detailed than that of the Court of Appeals, it afforded a better vantage point from which to view the reasoning that led to Gautier's defeat. Judge Shientag spoke for the majority.

After stating the facts of the case and quoting from the Civil Rights Law, Judge Shientag observed that past applications of the privacy statute indicated a more liberal treatment of claims in cases based on uses "for advertising purposes" than in cases concerned with uses "for trade purposes." Advertising matter was easy to spot. Looking at the printed page, one would find such matter blocked off from other matter. So that ordinarily any name or picture found within the confines of advertising space would be considered used for advertising purposes. However, the purpose for which a name or picture is used outside of advertising space is not readily detectable. And in our zeal to fulfill the "compelling public interest in the free flow of ideas" we tend to play down any notions that such use is "for purposes of trade."

On what basis was the claim of invasion made in the *Gautier* case? The plaintiff contended that the use of his name and picture in the telecast was a use for advertising purposes. Hence he was calling upon the court to apply the liberal treatment. But the court did not agree that the commercial sponsorship of television programs rendered the use of names and pictures therein a use for advertising purposes. Said Judge Shientag:

> The unique economic necessities of radio and television, however, require that, in large part, programs appear under the sponsorship of commercial advertisers. To hold that the mere fact of sponsorship makes the unauthorized use of an individual's name or picture on radio or television a use "for advertising purposes" would materially weaken the informative and educational potentials of these still developing media. We hold, therefore, that in the absence of exploitation of a name or picture in the commerical announcement or in direct connection with the product itself, there is no use "for advertising purposes." . . . as the record makes clear that there was here no such exploitation of plaintiff's name or picture, plaintiff cannot recover under this aspect of the Civil Rights Law.

Having disposed of the argument that plaintiff's name and picture had been used for advertising purposes, Judge Shientag undertook to answer what he called the "more difficult question" as to whether or not there had been a use for trade purposes. If the portrayal of the plaintiff were in connection with the dissemination of news there would be no difficulty in concluding that it was immune from attack. On the other hand, if the portrayal were fictional, an opposite conclusion would be reached with equal ease. But the televising of plaintiff's act was neither a dissemination of news nor a fictionalized treatment of news. It, therefore, lay somewhere between the two and could not be left to straddle the line of demarcation. The learned judge laid out the problem:

> Between these two extremes of news and fiction lies a vast middle ground which is neither one nor the other. In determining whether recovery should be granted in such cases, no hard and fast rules can be laid down— at any rate not at this stage of the development of the law on this subject. Necessarily, each case must be decided on a weighing of conflicting

policies: the public interest in free dissemination of information against the interest in the preservation of the inviolate personality. Among the relevant factors in such decision are the media used, the nature of the subject matter and the extent of the actual invasion of privacy.

The question was difficult all right, but the problem of deciphering the logic of the court's opinion was doubly difficult. The court seemed to be grappling with a tangled mass of barbed wire. It had concluded that the answer sought lay not in the extremes but somewhere in the middle. To extract the solution required certain tools. These were laid out: media used; nature of the subject matter; and extent of invasion. Were these to be used separately or in combination? It seemed that the first two were used simultaneously.

The court first spoke of newspapers as having a "traditional function of news dissemination." Yet, newspapers have contained other matters pertaining to persons without incurring liability.

> Articles such as biographical narratives of a man's life when it is of legitimate public interest, and "travel stories, stories of distant places, tales of historic personages and events, the reproduction of items of past news, and surveys of social conditions" will generally be considered beyond the purview of the statute. . . ."

Could the same be said of other media? Said the court:

> In the main, this principle extends to the newsreel, the radio and to television.

So here were areas into which television could delve, along with newspapers, but the portrayal of Gautier did not fit the enumerated categories.

Next, the court dealt with subject matter that was meant solely for entertainment:

> Where, however, the subject matter is solely for entertainment purposes and particularly where it appears in a medium not identified, in the main, with the dissemination of news, recovery will be more freely permitted. In Redmond vs. Columbia Pictures Corp. . . ., plaintiff, a professional golfer and trick shot artist, gave, without compensation, a private exhibition of trick shots for the Fox Movietone News. Fox exhibited the film as part of a newsreel. Thereafter, the defendant purchased the film from Fox and incorporated it into a short, humorous feature film entitled *Golfing Rhythm*. A verdict for the plaintiff was upheld by this court and the Court of Appeals . . ."

For a further illustration the court referred to the *Colyer* case (discussed above) in which recovery was denied to a professional high diver whose picture appeared in the Police Gazette. Did the court mean that the *Police Gazette* was a medium "identified, in the main, with the dissemination of news?" As a final illustration in support of its point, referring to the *Humiston* case (discussed above), the court said:

> It has been indicated that the broadcast of a parade or a sporting event, such as a football game, would be placed outside the statute . . .

It should be made clear that that case had nothing to do with a parade or a sporting event, and that what Judge Shientag was doing was merely reiterating a thought expressed by the judge who rendered the decision in that case.

What Judge Shientag had to say about entertainment turned out to be surplusage, for it was not his purpose to tie in pure entertainment with a medium identified with the dissemination of news. The tie-in was to be between the entertainment of Gautier and "a public event of general interest." Since the case fell into an intermediate category between news and fiction, he continued: "It becomes necessary then to examine the particular facts before us to determine whether the privilege accorded to news and matters of public interest should be extended to cover the instant case."

It could not be denied that Gautier's act was purely entertainment, and that its transmission to the public through television was for the purpose of furnishing entertainment. The learned judge's discussion of uses for entertainment purposes was neither here nor there. He did not say that such use by a medium identified with the dissemination of news was entirely free from attack. But the entertainment had been performed in connection with a football game. Was a football game a matter of public interest? Why could not the entertainment be considered part of that event? The judicial mind found the answer:

> Plaintiff's act, while basically for the purpose of entertainment, was televised in connection with a public event of general interest. It appeared through a medium which affords unique opportunities of public import, a medium which should not be confined by too restricted a delineation of the permissible scope of its operation.

And so the court was satisfied with the first two categories of the three-pronged test it had set out to apply. Television was considered to be a medium for the dissemination of news and hence "not precluded by section 51 of the Civil Rights Law from publishing or depicting matters of public interest." Secondly, the subject matter was a public event of general interest, since it was televised in connec-

tion with such an event. The third prong, the extent of the actual
invasion of privacy, had yet to be discussed.

Suppose it were conceded that the plaintiff's right of privacy was
invaded. To what extent could it be said to have been invaded?
Enough to bother about? The court felt that "the extent of the impingement on plaintiff's privacy would in this case seem to be minimal." "There was," said the court, "no substantial invasion of plaintiff's 'right to be let alone' in telecasting an act voluntarily performed
by plaintiff for pay before 35,000 spectators."

Thus the third prong was set in place. But the court was not satisfied that its job was complete. The three prongs were not sharply
pointed. Television as a medium for the dissemination of news was
not exactly in the same class as the newspaper. Entertainment performed at a football game was not exactly a matter of general public
interest. Though not substantial, an invasion was nevertheless an
invasion. Something more had to be added before turning the plaintiff out of court. Was the plaintiff really interested in his privacy, or
was he not rather interested in his business? Was not the privacy statute
aimed at protecting the individual against encroachments upon his
person rather than against injuries to his business? Well then, the
plaintiff was simply barking up the wrong tree. It was such thinking
that produced the following statement:

> In the light of the history of section 51 and its subsequent judicial in-
> terpretations, it is clear that this statute was never intended to apply to
> cases like the instant one. The statutory creation in this State of a lim-
> ited right of privacy was intended for the protection of the personality
> of an individual against unlawful invasion. . . . It provided primarily a
> recovery for injury to the person, not to his property or business. The
> recovery is grounded on the mental strain and distress, on the humilia-
> tion, on the disturbance of the peace of mind suffered by the individual
> affected. True, where an individual's right of privacy has been invaded
> there are certain other elements which may be taken into consideration
> in assessing the damages. Thus, where a cause of action under the civil
> rights statute has been established, damages may include recovery for a
> so-called "property" interest inherent and inextricably interwoven in
> the individual's personality . . ., but it is the injury to the person, not
> the property, which establishes the cause of action. That is the focal
> point of the statute.

The foregoing opinion adds a strange twist to previous applications
of the New York privacy statute. Here is a case which seems to involve
all the ingreditents of invasion, as specified in the statute, and yet the
court has managed, by careful reasoning, to place the situation beyond
the prohibited area.

Judge Desmond, who voted with the majority of the Court of Appeals when that court upheld the decision of the Appellate Division, said in his concurring opinion: "It seems to me that the televising of plaintiff's act was, in undisputable fact, a use thereof 'for advertising purposes,' without plaintiff's consent." Yet, the learned judge was not satisfied that the statute had been violated, for he went on to say: "But that does not end this case. My difficulty is that there was no invasion of any 'right of privacy'." Why did Judge Desmond think there was no invasion of privacy in this case? Because Gautier was a professional entertainer, and "privacy is the one thing he did not want, or need, in his occupation." Like Judge Shientag of the Appellate Division, he felt that Gautier's real grievance was not the invasion of his privacy but "that he was not paid for the telecasting of his show."

Although the New York statute is captioned "Right of Privacy," that expression can nowhere be found within the text of sections 50 and 51. The legislature did not designate the right of privacy as a property right or as a personal right. The statute did not state its purpose to be the protection of personality or the desire to be let alone. It did not distinguish between persons who sought publicity and those who cherished privacy. It said nothing of occupations. It could very well be conceived of as intended to protect against exploitations as well as against exposures. The statute did not mention "mental strain and distress," "humiliation," or "the disturbance of the peace of mind suffered by the individual affected." If the legislature had intended to confine the scope of its enactment to such injuries alone, it could easily have done so. However, it spoke only of uses for "advertising" and "trade" purposes, and there should be no reason to doubt that the provision entitling victims to damages was meant to include both compensation for pain and suffering and compensation for unjust enrichment of the culprit, without the mental or contractual ground of recovery being made prerequisite to each other.

Judge Shientag observed that there was a middle ground between news and fiction, and that when a case fell into that area no hard and fast rules could be applied. In deciding such cases, he felt consideration should be given to "media used, the nature of the subject matter and the extent of the actual invasion of privacy." He went on to say that where "the subject matter is solely for entertainment purposes and particularly where it appears in a medium not identified, in the main, with the dissemination of news, recovery will be more freely permitted." Why, then, was recovery not freely permitted in this case? Could it reasonably be said that the subject matter was not "solely for entertainment purposes?" Could it reasonably be said that television was a medium "identified, in the main, with the dissemination of news?" The learned judge said that plaintiff's act, "while basically for the purpose of entertainment, was televised in connection with a public event of general interest?" Was not the whole show, including the "public event" (if we can regard a football game as a public event), a form of entertainment? And as to the medium, said the court: "It appeared through a medium which affords unique opportunities for the instantaneous dissemination of news and events of public import, a medium which should not be confined by too restricted a delineation of the permissible scope of its operation." That it affords unique opportunities for dissemination of news does not mean that television is, "in the main," identified with news dissemination. That there are opportunities for beneficent use of a medium does not preclude the possibility of abuse. To hold that the operator of any medium has violated the statute does not necessarily mean that its lawful scope of operation has been restricted.

As to the extent of the actual invasion in this case, Judge Shientag thought that it "would in this case seem to be minimal." Why? Because Gautier was performing before 35,000 spectators and was not interested, therefore, in privacy. Besides, his portrayal was factual, while those of Binns, the hero, and Redmond, the trick-shot artist, were fictionalized. Their privacies lay in their personalities, while Gautier's lay in his pocket-book. So felt the court. But again, let us repeat, the statute says nothing of personality or property, nor does it distinguish between fact and fiction. It speaks only of commercializing a person without his consent. If there is any connection between the title "Right of Privacy" and the statutory sections which follow it, there can be no denial that the legislative mind envisioned a commercial element in privacy.

Judge Froessel, who gave the opinion for the majority of the Court of Appeals, confined his reasoning to an evaluation of the portrayal in the light of its purpose. He found the portrayal to be justified on the basis that the performance was newsworthy. Included in his opinion was the statement:

> While one who is a public figure or is presently newsworthy may be the proper subject of news or informative presentation, the privilege does not extend to commercialization of his personality through a form of treatment distinct from the dissemination of news or information.

Was the performance of Gautier a matter of news, or did its presentation supply information? Did the learned judge mean that, unless fictionally portrayed, a public figure could be portrayed at any time with impunity, even though a particular portrayal had value only as entertainment? Surely Gautier was hired only for the purpose of entertaining the customers, and the entertainment was extended to a wider audience through television. Surely no one watching the show conceived of the performance as news, nor could anyone conceive that its purpose was to make those whose attention it attraced better informed.

Where is the line of demarcation that was drawn by the New York legislature fifty-five years ago? Have its interpretations reflected the concepts of Samuel Warren and Louis D. Brandeis? It lies somewhere in the now familiar area called "the twilight zone," into which people find it expedient to throw all difficult questions. It bears only the faint reflection of road-markers placed too far from the edge of a highway.

Conception in Georgia

Pavesich v. New England Life Ins. Co. (1905) was decided by the highest court of Georgia just three years after the *Roberson* decision in New York. The cases resembled each other in that both involved the use of a picture for advertising purposes. While Miss Roberson's picture was used to advertise flour, Pavesich's picture was used to advertise insurance. The picture appeared in a newspaper advertisement beside the picture of an ill-dressed and sickly looking person. The caption above plaintiff's picture read, "Do it now. The man who did." Above the other were the words, "Do it while you can. The man who didn't." Below both was the statement, "These two pictures tell their own story." Attributed to the plainiff was a statement to the effect that he had bought insurance from the defendant company during his productive years and that his family was amply protected. The other man was pictured as saying that he had failed to buy insurance and had come to realize his mistake. As a matter of fact, plaintiff had not dealt with defendant insurance company, had not made the statement attributed to him, nor had he consented to the publication of his picture. He based his case on an alleged invasion of his right of privacy. The court was well aware of the New York decision, the only other decision previously given by a court of last resort on the question of privacy. It was likewise aware of the article that had been written on the subject by Warren and Brandeis. The facts of the case were simple, leaving but one question for consideration. After reviewing the situation, the court put the matter this way:

> The question therefore to be determined is whether an individual has a right of privacy which he can enforce, and which the courts will protect against invasion. It is to be conceded that prior to 1890 every adjudicated case, both in this country and in England, which might be said to have involved a right of privacy, was not based upon the existence of such right, but was founded upon a supposed right of property, or a breach of trust or confidence, or the like, and that therefore a claim to a right of privacy, independent of a property or contractual right, or some right of a similar nature, had, up to that time, never been recognized in terms in any decision. The entire absence for a long period of time, even for centuries, of a precedent for an asserted right should have the effect to

75

cause the courts to proceed with caution before recognizing the right, for
fear that they may thereby invade the province of the lawmaking power;
but such absence, even for all time, is not conclusive of the question as
to the existence of the right. The novelty of the complaint is no objection, when an injury cognizable by law is shown to have been inflicted
on the plaintiff. In such a case, "although there be no precedent, the
common law will judge according to the law of nature and the public
good." Where the case is new in principle, the courts have no authority
to give a remedy, no matter how great the grievance; but where the case
is only new in instance, and the sole question is upon the application
of a recognized principle to a new case, "it will be just as competent to
courts of justice to apply the principle to any case that may arise two
centuries hence as it was two centuries ago." Broom's Legal Maxims
(8th Ed.) 193. This results from the application of the maxim, *Ubi jus ibi
remedium,* which finds expression in our Code, where it is declared that
"for every right there shall be a remedy, and every court having jurisdiction of the one may, if necessary, frame the other." Civ. Code 1895,
sec. 4929.

Thus did the Georgia court dispose of the argument, used by the
New York court, that there was no precedent for recognition of the
right asserted. On what basis then did the court recognize the right of
privacy?

The right of privacy within certain limits is a right derived from natural
law, recognized by the principles of municipal law, and guaranteed to
persons in this state by both the Constitutions of the United States and
of the state of Georgia, in those provisions which declare that no person
shall be deprived of liberty except by due process of law.

So the right of privacy is conceived of as arising out of natural law,
the law that lies at the base of human understanding concerning the
innate rights and duties of mankind, the law that is given expression in
the Declaration of Independence by the terms, "unalienable rights,"
"life," "liberty," and "the pursuit of happiness." What is more natural
than the desire of a human being to be master of himself, to be immune from subservience to the whims and exploitations of others?
Liberty encompasses the right to privacy just as it also affords freedom to publish. Both rights are subject to limitations, and the question
is not whether the first exists but, rather, to what exent each must
be restrained in order to give the broadest possible effect to the other.

The Georgia Constitution provides: "Any person may speak, write
and publish his sentiments on all subjects, being responsible for the
abuse of that liberty."

How far then may one go in exercising the right of free speech with
impunity? The Georgia court gave its answer in these words:

... To make intelligent, forceful, and effective an expression of opinion, it may be necessary to refer to the life, conduct, and character of a person; and, so long as the truth is adhered to, the right of privacy of another cannot be said to have been invaded by one who speaks or writes or prints, provided the reference to such person, and the manner in which he is referred to, is reasonably and legitimately proper in an expression of opinion on the subject that is under investigation. . . . The truth may be spoken, written, or printed about all matters of a public nature, as well as matters of a private nature in which the public has a legitimate interest. The truth may be uttered and printed in reference to the life, character, and conduct of individuals whenever it is necessary to the full exercise of the right to express one's sentiments on any and all subjects that may be proper matter for discussion.

The principle derived from the foregoing observation is that the right of privacy is not to be considered violated by truthful expressions concerning a person in connection with matters in which the public has a legitimate interest. Whether or not the public has a legitimate interest may in some cases be difficult to determine. The Georgia court felt, however, that the difficulty in drawing a line between private and public interests does not justify the denial of relief where it is clearly shown that a wrong has been committed. The court found no difficulty in applying its conception of privacy to the situation presented in the *Pavesich* case.

How has privacy been treated in Georgia since 1905? Although the reported cases are not nearly as numerous as the New York cases, they represent an interesting variety.

In 1924, a case arose out of the happenings aboard a vessel at sea. The husband of the plaintiff had left their stateroom temporarily, and the plaintiff had gone to bed, when the defendant entered the room without invitation. The door had been closed and the lights turned out. He proceeded to tear the bedclothing off her, disheveled her nightclothes, grabbed her in his arms, and sought to get in bed with her, as the court put it, "for the purpose of debauching her." She screamed. Her husband returned. A fight ensued. When action was brought, the judge charged the jury that the basis on which a finding favorable to the plaintiff might be arrived at was assault and battery, and that no action would lie upon the ground that defendant had entered the stateroom. The Appellate Court decided that this charge was erroneous, saying that passengers on vessels were entitled to the privacy of their rooms, and that any improper, unjustified, or unreasonable intrusion constituted a proper ground for action. Here is privacy in its most intimate state, and it would have been a pity if a less aggressive intruder had been allowed to make his entrance with impunity. Yet, we shall later see an altogether different treatment of a somewhat similar situation by the court of another state.

In 1930, the Georgia court applied the doctrine of privacy in a manner born of extraordinary conception. The male child of the plaintiffs had come into this world with his heart outside of his body. A corrective operation proved unsuccessful, and the child died. The hospital allowed a photographer to photograph and portray the child in a nude condition. The photographer gave the picture to the Savannah Press, and the picture was published together with a story of the oddity. Claiming to have been shocked, humiliated, and made sick by the publication of the picture, the parents brought action against the hospital, the photographer, and the newspaper publisher for invasion of their right of privacy. The lower court sustained a demurrer interposed by the defendants, but the upper court reversed this decision, saying that in its opinion the plaintiffs had stated a cause of action. It should be especially noted that this court recognized an invasion of the privacy of persons other than the individual whose features were exposed to public view. Two dissenting judges felt that the court was going too far in its conception of the right of privacy. They could not see how the exposure of the dead child had any connection with the privacy of the parents, and certainly a corpse, in their view, could not claim that its privacy had been invaded. But is there not some reflection cast upon the parents of such a child, and is there not some feeling of unity between parent and child, so that an unwarranted exposure of the one is equivalent to an unauthorized intrusion upon the seclusion preferred by the other?

Another example of a possible connection between the exposure of one deceased and the privacy of living persons may be found in *Schumann v. Loew's Incorporated* (1954), a New York case. In that case the great-grandchildren of Robert Schumann, the famous composer who had died in 1856, claimed that their privacy had been invaded by the picture, *Song of Love,* which portrayed the life of Schumann, including the mental illness which overcame him and from which he suffered until his death. Not only were the plaintiffs anxious to protect the memory of their ancestor, but they were equally interested in protecting themselves against the impressions which might possibly be created by the picture in the mind of its viewers. The court could not recognize any right of the deceased to receive protection, since the New York statute specifically confined its scope to living persons. As for the possible effect of the exposure upon descendants of the deceased, the court could not see that the privacy of anyone but the deceased could possibly be in question, and certainly no one except the person whose privacy had been invaded could assert such right.

While the Georgia court, in 1930, took a dim view of what it considered an unwarranted exposure, the same court, in 1956, took a different view of another situation. This time the parents of a murdered child brought suit for an injunction and for the recovery of damages when a newspaper sold photographs showing the body of the murdered child. The court felt that the murder of a child was a matter of public interest, and that the publication of the photograph was justified on that basis. What possible benefit could the public derive from a view of the corpse? Were not the parents of this child as equally entitled to the veil of privacy as were the parents of the deformed child? Could not a consideration of the public interest have prevented a recovery in 1930? Could it be that our present conceptions of public interest have so enlarged its scope that privacy lingers at the fringe of the horizon? It must be admitted that courts are faced with quite a problem when privacy is involved, as witness the following case.

The case presents a truly amazing situation. A woman spent twenty-six days in a hospital. She occupied a private room. The Atlanta Coca-Cola Bottling Company had a receiving set installed in the room, with earphones located in the room directly above. Agents of the company were thereby enabled to listen in on and record conversations between the woman and her husband, as well as conversations with doctors and nurses. On the basis of these facts, action was brought against the company for the invasion of her right of privacy. The defendant admitted the truth of plaintiff's allegations, but submitted additional facts in an attempt to justify its eavesdropping. According to the defendant, the plaintiff was in the hospital for the purpose of building up a case of negligence against the company. She had bought a bottle of coca-cola at a store and nonchalantly stood by sipping the contents, taking her time to await an opportune moment. After drinking about one-third the way down, she caught the eye of the clerk as he gazed in her direction and began to cry out that glass was sticking in her throat and strangling her. She was taken to the hospital, where examining physicians found no signs of glass. But somehow or other pieces of broken glass were found in her bed pan. This, contended the defendant, was as fraudulent as her attempt to raise her temperature by holding a thermometer against a hot water bottle while her nurse's back was turned. During her stay in the hospital, she was visited by attorneys retained by the company to investigate her claim of injuries allegedly suffered from the swallowing of glass. She was anxious for a settlement and told them they could make any investigation they pleased. The defendant contended that this amounted to authority to make its informative installation. The court did not agree, and yet it affirmed the judgment given by the lower court in favor of the defendant. The appeal was taken on the ground that the lower court had erred in admitting evidence obtained by eavesdropping. The upper court felt that such evidence was admissible "in extenuation or mitigation of damages." This means that such evidence could be submitted for the purpose of reducing the amount of damage to which a party might otherwise be entitled. According to the reasoning of the court, it seems that the judgment should have been rendered in favor of the plaintiff, even if she had to come away with no more than nominal damages (a token amount). Regardless of the scheme allegedly perpetrated by the plaintiff, the court felt that the defendant had acted without permission and had committed an invasion of privacy. But while the contentions of the defendant, if believed, could have the effect of reducing, or even extinguishing, the amount of recoverable damages, they could not extinguish her right of action. Yet, judgment in this case went to the defendant. There are many cases in which parties succeed in winning judgments, by establishing violations of their rights, but fail in their attempts to obtain substantial damages. On the other hand, a more serious question is presented by this case.

Is a skeptical potential defendant justified in seeking to obtain evidence by intruding upon the privacy of his potential adversary? If this question is answered in the affirmative, such conclusion would have to be arrived at through the application of the principle that the end justifies the means. Yet such a principle is foreign to the thinking of freedom-loving peoples. If the question is answered in the negative, then why should evidence thereby obtained be allowed to minimize the effect of the injury sustained? The basis upon which recovery for invasion of privacy is allowed in Georgia is the injury to the sensibilities of the victim. Surely the injury is not reduced by facts related to matters other than the invasion itself, and to give effect to evidence obtained by wrongdoing is to justify the wrong. No wrong is justified, for what is considered justified is right and not wrong. If it is wrong, the culprit ought not to benefit from it, but the victim is entitled to redress for the suffering inflicted by the wrongdoer. To allow a person to benefit from his wrong is to encourage a practice sought to be eliminated.

The bounds of privacy grow narrower while we continue to profess respect for its realm. Creditors sometimes use questionable methods in attempting to procure payments from their debtors, thereby provoking cries of invasion. A relatively recent Georgia case illustrates one such method and its evaluation by the court in relation to the right of privacy.

The defendant, a finance company, sent two telegrams to the plaintiff within four days. The first read: "Must have March payment immediately or legal action." The second read: "Payments must be received by Monday or legal action." A cursory view of this situation might lead one to utter: "So what?" What bothered the plaintiff was the fact that the finance company had chosen to communicate with him in a semi-public way, a way which could lead to a broadcast of what he considered his private affairs. Could not the same object have been accomplished through a more private medium? Was not this method chosen in order to exert that little extra pressure that comes from fear of wide knowledge? The plaintiff brought action for libel and for invasion of his privacy.

The libel action was dismissed on two grounds. First, there was no allegation that the words were used in reference to the business, profession, or trade of the plaintiff. Second, there was no allegation to the effect that plaintiff was engaged in a vocation requiring credit. It was alleged that plaintiff was a pipe-cutter, that he followed construction work, and that he had to pay his debts and have a good credit standing in order to obtain employment. The court held that this was not an allegation to the effect that plaintiff required credit in his pipe-cutting and construction business in order to carry on such business.

As for the claim that his privacy had been invaded, the court said:

> On this basis no cause of action is set forth because it is plain that a creditor has a perfect right to send a debtor a telegram in good faith and threaten legal action if the default continues. If such a communication is not actionable the fact that no debt was due and the actor acted in bad faith would not make the cause of action good on the ground of a violation of the right of privacy. There is still another reason, (and there may be more), and that is that the protection afforded by the law to the right of privacy must be restricted to "ordinary sensibilities" and not to supersensitiveness or agoraphobia. . . . There are some shocks, inconveniences and annoyancies which members of society in the nature of things must absorb without the right of redress. It would seem that one who was billed by mistake would know of the mistake or could discover it, and that a publication to a few employees of a telegraph company who are not alleged to be acquainted with the alleged injured party would not offend the sensibilities of a person who has gone into debt and subjected himself to the standard communications of a civilized society.

Thus, in Georgia, the conception of unlawful invasion of privacy seems to be confined to those instances in which the intrusion is offensive to the sensibilities of ordinary individuals. While the intrusion in some cases may seem trivial, and while it may appear that the feelings of persons having ordinary sensibilities would not be affected, a little encouragement can lead intruders to venture even further into seemingly forbidden territory. It would seem that our creditor could have communicated his impatience in a more private way, thereby sparing the alleged debtor any possible feeling of embarrassment. There are areas in the law where judgments are based upon a contemplation of the so-called ordinary, prudent, or reasonable, person. On the other hand, the injury to one person is not to be determined, either in fact or in extent, by what a stronger person might have withstood. The concept of invasion of privacy as an injury to feelings is a narrow one. Of course, the effect upon the feelings of an individual should be considered, but it is equally important to recognize privacy as a domain, over which the individual is master, and within whose borders there must be no unjustifiable trespass. When injuries to property give rise to action, the feelings of the victim are not counted in the measurement of damages, nor is injury to feelings prerequisite to recovery. When bodily injuries are suffered, the victim is allowed damages for pain and suffering in addition to actual losses incurred and to be incurred on account of the injury. Cannot privacy be considered both a personal and a property right? Thus, the invasion itself would be considered a wrong, and the effect upon the feelings would be only one element to be considered in the assessment of damages.

It is beginning to appear that Georgia is advancing toward this suggested view. The latest case decided in that state gives some indication of a tendency toward a broader concept of privacy. *Gouldman-Taber Pontiac v. Zerbst* (1957) involved another method used by creditors to facilitate the collection of debts. The Pontiac Company, defendant, had performed certain repair services for the plaintiff, after which a dispute arose as to the repair bill. Finding that plaintiff was employed by Lockheed Aircraft Corporation, defendant wrote a letter to plaintiff's employer. Statements made in the letter were to the following effect: that the letter was being written regarding one who was a customer of defendant and an employee of Lockheed; that defendant was reluctant to write to employers of its customers, but was doing so as a last resort; that every effort had been made to achieve an amicable settlement, but that the customer was not cooperative; and that any assistance on the part of the employer in bringing about the termination of "an honest debt" incurred by the customer would be appreciated. Plaintiff stated in her complaint that, upon receipt of the letter, one of her supervisors called her in, questioned her, and told her that the letter would be placed in the permanent file of personal data and would not be removed until receipt of further communication evidencing a settlement of the claim. Plaintiff also alleged that, as a result of defendant's willful, intentional, and malicious attack on her good name and character, she was humiliated, embarrassed, and upset; that her peace of mind, happiness, and feelings were wounded; that she suffered great mental pain and distress; and that defendant's act constituted an invasion of her privacy. The defendant demurred. The demurrer was overruled. The defendant appealed. The decision was affirmed.

The decision seemed to hinge on the fact that the debt was in dispute. Since the debt had not yet been established by a judgment rendered by a court of law, it was of no concern to the employer of the alleged debtor. The relationship between the plaintiff and her employer was equally of no concern to the alleged creditor. If the debt had been established, the employer could have been brought into the picture through garnishment proceedings. By such proceedings, an employer is ordered by the court to withhold a portion of the debtor's wages and to make such portion available toward the extinction of the judgment debt. In such case, the affairs of the employee would become known to the employer anyway, and any solicitation of assistance from the employer by the creditor would not be deemed an invasion of privacy. Such solicitation before judgment, however, infringes upon the freedom to which the employee is entitled in negotiating a settlement or defending against a possibly false claim.

This latest decision of the Georgia court differed in at least one respect from the decision given previously in a case involving the conduct of a creditor. The 1957 decision did not discuss the effect of the action taken by the creditor upon the feelings of the debtor. The opinion was concerned, in the main, with the propriety of the defendant's act rather than with the mental effect of such act. Whether such act would affect persons of ordinary sensibilities was not discussed as a question to be decided. Perhaps this aspect of the case was taken for granted. Perhaps the scope of privacy in Georgia is now somewhat broader than originally conceived.

We have taken special note of the Georgia cases because the Georgia Supreme Court was the first court of last resort to recognize the right of privacy as a common law right. In contrast, we found a denial of such right by the New York Court of Appeals three years earlier. While the stature of privacy has continued to grow in Georgia, the same cannot be said of its treatment in New York. The New York conception has a strictly commercial flavor; that of Georgia respects the dignity of the individual and approaches the idea of an inviolate personality.

7

Invasion by Advertising

We have already seen that the use of a person's name or picture, without his consent, is considered an invasion of privacy under the common law of Georgia and under the statutory law of New York. Let us now tour the other states in which claims of invasion have arisen from use of names and pictures in advertising matter. We shall witness a greater variety of situations as well as contrasting lines of treatment.

Rhode Island's contribution to the subject of privacy comes from the case of *Henry v. Cherry & Webb* (1909). The defendants were merchants engaged in the business of selling dry goods, ladies' garments, and other articles of clothing. Their advertisement in the *Providence Evening Bulletin* contained a picture of the plaintiff driving a car in which others were passengers. The caption indicated that the advertisement was for the purpose of promoting the sales of auto coats. The plaintiff complained that he thereby became the object of scoffs, ridicule, public comment, gibes by friends and acquaintances, and that he was caused great mental anguish. The court held that there was no such thing as a right of privacy in Rhode Island.

According to the Rhode Island court, the laws of a state consist of the rules and enactments of the legislature as well as long-established local customs having the force of law. It would be difficult to quarrel with this conception of the law, but was it customary for merchants in Rhode Island to make use of suitable photographs without challenge? Might it not have been customary for merchants to refrain from such uses out of regard for what they considered to be the undeniable rights of individuals? The court looked for a line of cases recognizing the right and found none. So it turned to legislation and found the word "liberty," as used in the Constitution of the United States and of Rhode Island, the only possible repository of such right. Would this suffice as it did in Georgia? The court rejected the Georgia view, for it felt that the Constitutional sections referring to liberty were borrowed from the Great Charter (Magna Carta), wherein the freedom of freemen was spoken of in terms of immunity from arrest, imprisonment, disseizin, outlawry, punishment, and destruction, rather than in terms commensurate with notions of privacy. The court also rejected the connection contrived by promoters of privacy between privacy and the now famous words expressed by Cooley, "the right to be let alone." These words, according to the court, were used by Cooley in reference to freedom from bodily harm and the fear of bodily harm, rather than in espousement of a right to be free from public comment.

It matters not with what intention Cooley originally expressed these famous words. The fact that they were expressed would indicate his recognition of a "right to be let alone." And surely such right would include immunity from all sorts of encroachments.

Except where the existence of a right of privacy is emphatically denied, such as in Rhode Island, the great majority of cases involving the use of names or pictures in advertising matter have been decided in favor of the complaining parties. Some of the violations are so flagrant that contrary conclusions are hardly imaginable.

During his early career, Thomas Edison compounded a medicinal preparation which was intended for the relief of neuralgic pains through external application. He sold his rights in the preparation for $5,000. Subsequent successive sales placed the preparation in the hands of an organization which chose to call itself the Edison Polyform Manufacturing Company. They manufactured a liquid preparation containing all the ingredients of the original except morphine, and they put a label on the bottle. The label consisted of a picture of Edison and the following words: "Edison's Polyform. I certify that this preparation is compounded according to the formula devised and used by myself. Thos. A. Edison." Edison sought an injunction against the use of his name in this fashion. The injunction was granted. The year was 1907. The state was New Jersey.

In 1909, a Kentucky Court struck down the use of a picture and forged letter as an endorsement, by a prominent citizen, of Doan's Kidney Pills. But in 1952, in the same state, a cute but questionable advertising device proved harmless to its perpetrator. The defendant operated a retail clothing store in Louisville. In promotion of a sale, a series of postcards were mailed to prospective customers. One such card, in feminine handwriting, was addressed to the plaintiff. It contained these words: "Please call WAbash 1492 and ask for Carolyn." Since men are usually away at work when mail is delivered to their homes, the card meant for the plaintiff found itself in the hands of his wife. She immediately became upset and she awaited his homecoming with burning impatience. "Who is Carolyn?" she wanted to know.

To prove his fidelity, the plaintiff lifted the receiver and dialed the number. Of course, by that time the store was closed, so it was no wonder that no one answered. And of course, the flame of rage that rose from her imagination now completely enveloped the wife and she exploded through the door, leaving the plaintiff to ponder his predicament. His wife was gone. His home was wrecked. What was left for him to do but to seek redress from him who had caused such grief? He brought action. But the court refused to give him relief. The court found it difficult to believe that a contented wife would leave her husband on such meager evidence and fail to return even after all the facts were revealed. And to show what it thought of plaintiff's case, the court said:

> Modern day advertising techniques have come to be accepted and are in effect a limitation on the individual's right of privacy. Such methods are not actionable so long as they are not unreasonable.

We are supposed to believe that a postcard containing nothing but the words quoted above is a reasonable method of advertising. We are also supposed to agree that it is vain for one to seek salvation while others surrender to the outstretched claws of unbridled and oblivious operators.

Munden v. Harris (1911) left no doubt as to Missouri's view of privacy. This is another case involving an advertising stunt. The defendants were jewelry merchants. The plaintiff was a five-year-old child. To advertise their merchandise, the defendants published a picture of the plaintiff together with the following statement falsely attributed to the plaintiff:

> Papa is going to buy Mamma an Elgin watch for a present and some one (I mustn't tell who) is going to buy my big sister a diamond ring. So don't you think you ought to buy me something? The payments are so easy, you'll never miss the money if you get it of
> > Harris-Goar Co.
> > 1207 Grand Ave.
> > Kansas City, Mo.
>
> Gifts for Everybody
> Everywhere in their
> Free Catalogue

The Missouri court was faced with the problem of deciding what way to lean on the question of privacy. It recognized the right and considered an invasion of privacy not as an injury to feelings but as an injury to property. Said the court:

Property is not necessarily a taxable thing any more than it is always a tangible thing. It may consist of things incorporeal, and things incorporeal may consist of rights common in every man. One is not compelled to show that he used, or intended to use any right which he has, in order to determine whether it is a valuable right of which he cannot be deprived, and in which the law will protect him. . . . One may have peculiarity of appearance, and if it is to be made a matter of merchandise, why should it not be for his benefit? It is a right which he may wish to exercise for his own profit, and why may he not restrain another who is using it for gain? If there is value in it, sufficient to excite the cupidity of another, why is it not the property of him who gives it the value and from whom the value springs?

The court was quick to add a qualification to its description of a picture as the subject of an exclusive property right:

It ought, however, to be added that though a picture is property, its owner, of course, may consent to its being used by others. This consent may be expressed, or it may be shown by acts which would be inconsistent with the claim of exclusive use, as if one should become a man engaged in public affairs, or who, by a course of conduct, has excited public interest.

This qualification is not to be taken as a justification of any use of a public figure's picture for advertising purposes. It obviously refers to the inclusion of such picture in commentaries upon matters of public interest. It did not pertain to the Munden child. He won his case.

In 1918, Kansas was added to the list of states that recognized the right of privacy concerning another advertising stunt. With no knowledge of what was going on, a woman, while shopping in a dry goods store, became the subject of a motion picture. The camera moved up and down to gather in everything about her. The picture was then exhibited at a local movie house to advertise the defendant's business. She brought action, claiming that she had become the subject of common talk throughout the community, it being believed that she had been hired for her performance. The court held that the facts alleged by her constituted a cause of action.

The manner in which the right of privacy is recognized in Kansas is made clear in *Johnson v. Boeing Airplane Co.* (1953) . Johnson was employed as a sheet-metal worker. He was asked to pose with others as they were working on a plane. He made no objection. The picture taken at that time was later used in advertising matter designed to promote sales of planes manufactured by Boeing. When Johnson found out that the picture had been used in that way, he brought action for invasion of his privacy, citing *Kunz v. Allen,* the 1918 decision, in support of his claim. The court decided in favor of the defendant. Concerning plaintiff's contention that he was entitled to relief on the basis cf the *Kunz* case, the court said:

> The distinction between the facts of this case and those of the *Kunz* case . . . are too obvious to require elaboration and discussion.

That the distinction is obvious is no reason for ignoring the similarity. The plaintiffs in both cases were portrayed in advertising matter without consent. Did the difference lie in the fact that one was a customer while the other was an employee? Are we sure that what the court had to say about Johnson was not equally true of Mrs. Kunz? The court gave this estimate of Johnson's case:

> Plaintiff's evidence clearly discloses that he was not hurt, embarrassed, humiliated, aggravated, or in any way "put out," due to the publication of the advertisement. His subsequent "feeling" in the matter arose when, after being "kidded" by a few of his friends and relatives, he concluded that he should have been compensated. It is clear that his subsequent irritation was the result of his not being compensated, rather than because of the publication of the advertisement, and that the entire matter was an "afterthought" on his part. To permit recovery under these facts would expand the doctrine of privacy beyond all logical reasoning and stretch it almost to the point of absurdity.

Thus, we see that the recognition of the right of privacy in Kansas is based upon the theory that an invasion consists of an injury to feelings. Contrast this with the property theory adopted in Missouri. Consider whether the loyalties owed by employees are so great that they may be freely utilized by their employers in gaining benefits over and above those derived from the ordinary tasks which employees agree to undertake and perform. The advantage taken is the real invasion; the injury to feelings is but a consequence.

While Massachusetts has not denied that a right of privacy exists, none of its reported cases has been decided in favor of any plaintiff who has complained of an invasion. In 1921, Wallace Marek, fourteen years old, began selling goods bought from the Zanol Products Company. His sales were made as the result of house to house canvassing in the neighborhood in which he lived. Who would not patronize this needy neighborhood boy? None but the heartless. And so his business grew. He was persistent and progressive. In a few years, he purchased a truck and set up a store for the purpose of expanding the business. In 1927, he won a sales contest and was requested to submit a photograph and a letter for publication in the *Zanol Hustler,* whose

25,000 copies were distributed monthly among Zanol representatives, to pep them up, and among prospective representatives, to recruit their services. The process was repeated in the February, 1930, issue. But later, between July, 1930, and August, 1932, Marek's picture and letter were published in popular magazines having a national circulation, together with the following message: "Here is a picture of 21-year-old Wallace Marek who has often made $100 a week working for me. Send me your name and I will make you the same offer that started him on the road to success." Although he had furnished his picture and letter willingly, he had no idea that they would be used in this way. When Marek brought action in 1933, he claimed that his prominent display in national magazines caused his customers to feel that he was now too prosperous to need their business—that his large earnings indicated excessive profits. His business dropped sharply, and he gave up the store in 1931. He went back to canvassing and continued in this fashion until February, 1933. He was then sent to various cities for training as a branch manager. In April, 1933, he was made branch manager in the Trenton area, but gave up after six weeks and went back to canvassing. His action against Zanol products was commenced in December, 1933, and a final decision was reached by the Supreme Judicial Court of Massachusetts in 1937. Judgment was rendered in favor of the defendant. If there exists in Massachusetts a right of privacy, it is in no way indicated by this case.

As with other stunts, advertising stunts are not always successful; witness *Kerby v. Hal Roach Studios,* a California case decided in 1942. The plaintiff was Marion Kerby, an actress, concert singer, and monologist of many years experience both at home and abroad. The action arose as the result of what appears to have been a coincidence and its resulting consequences. Defendant, producer of motion pictures, thought of a scheme for promoting attendance at a theater in Los Angeles where one of its pictures was being shown. The chief character in the production was called Marion Kerby. It was not contended that this character was meant to portray the plaintiff, but what plaintiff complained of was the effect upon her of the advertising stunt concocted by the defendant. Pursuant to its plan, defendant prepared a letter written in a feminine hand and mechanically reproduced one thousand copies on pink stationery. The pink letters were inserted in pink envelopes addressed in a feminine hand to one thousand male householders. Here is the letter:

Dearest:
    Don't breathe it to a soul but I'm back in Los Angeles and more curious

than ever to see you. Remember how I cut up about a year ago? Well, I'm raring to go again, and believe me I'm in the mood for fun.

Let's renew our acquaintanceship and I promise you an evening you won't forget. Meet me in front of Warners Downtown Theatre at 7th and Hill on Thursday. Just look for a girl with a gleam in her eye, a smile on her lips and mischief on her mind!

Fondly,
Your ectoplasmic playmate,
Marion Kerby

How did this affect the plaintiff? She happened to live in Los Angeles and was the only person by that name listed in the city and telephone directories. As a result—well, let the court tell the story:

> The effects of the sending of this letter in the manner and to the persons above described are not depicted in the record except by an excluded offer of proof and a showing that plaintiff had a large number of telephone calls and a personal visit in regard to it; but no evidence and little imagination and knowledge of human nature are necessary to enable anyone to undertsand what results should be expected. It could not but lead to misunderstandings between husbands and wives who saw the letter and put the worst interpretation on it; it would arouse the expectations of lonesome males who were interested in the promised evening; and it must result in telephone calls and other communications from both irate wives and lonesome males and perhaps also from aggrieved but innocent husbands.

Aside from the possible effect the scheme might have on her reputation, the plaintiff became terribly excited, nervous, and unhappy. She was left with a feeling of disgrace and anguish, looking to the future with despair. In the case of any lady caller, she was seized with a fear of being shot.

Another court might have said that this sort of thing could be expected under modern methods of operation; that plaintiff should have realized her unintended role in the coincidental situation; that those who knew her would have recognized the error; and that a person of ordinary sensibilities would not have been affected. But the California court held that her right of privacy had been invaded.

In a 1955 case, the California court showed itself to be aligned with those courts that have considered an invasion of privacy to consist of an injury to feelings. In that case, the plaintiff, an attorney, had bought and later returned some photocopy equipment, but his name was included in a list of satisfied customers. The list was widely distributed throughout the United States. Said the court:

The gist of the cause of action in a privacy case is not injury to the character or reputation, but a direct wrong of a personal character resulting in injury to the feelings without regard to any effect which the publication may have on the property, business, pecuniary interest, or the standing of the individual in the community . . . The right of privacy concerns one's own peace of mind, while the right of freedom from defamation concerns primarily one's reputation. . . . The injury is mental and subjective. It impairs the mental peace and comfort of the person and may cause suffering much more acute than that caused by a bodily injury. . . . . The desire of a business concern for publicity or advertising does not justify its invasion of the right of privacy.

The court went on to say that an invasion brought about through error was nonetheless an invasion, and that the difficulty of proving damages should not be allowed to obliterate the wrong.

Advertising comes in many forms, the object being to attract customers. Whatever will attract the eyes of possible consumers is advantageously portrayed and prominently displayed. Brewers have found a fertile field for the sale of beer among sports enthusiasts. There was no television in 1942, the year in which *O'Brien v. Pabst Sales Co.* was decided by the United States Circuit Court of Appeals (fifth circuit). Among the methods used by Pabst to advertise its product was, and perhaps still is, the distribution of calendars bearing advertising matter. To assure their reception, use, and display, football schedules and pictures of star players were included. Davey O'Brien was a famous star, first as a student at Texas Christian University, and then in professional ranks. Of course his picture had been taken and publicized many times by public relations departments. But did that give Pabst the right to use his name and picture for the purpose of advertising beer? Two of the three judges felt that he had lost his right of privacy when he consented to wide publicity, and that he suffered no injury when the publicity department of his college authorized the particular publication upon which his action was based. To say that one who consents to wide publicity thereby waives all right with respect to his privacy and renders himself lawfully vulnerable to exploitation by any who choose to utilize his name and features does not seem logical.

The highest court of Michigan took a different view in a case bearing some marks of resemblance to the *O'Brien* case. Bernice Pallas, a showgirl in the employ of Earl Carroll, famous theatrical producer, consented to her being photographed for publicity purposes connected with the business of her employer. The owner of a retail department store in Detroit procured a copy of the picture from the photographer and had it published in connection with a newspaper advertisement designed to promote the sale of cosmetics. When action was brought, the defendant moved for dismissal on the basis of *Aktinson v. Doherty,* a case decided in Michigan many years before and referred to in our discussion of the *Roberson* case in Chapter IV. The lower court decided in favor of the defendant, but the upper court reversed the order of dismissal, refusing to follow the *Atkinson* case to the extent that it denied the existence of a right of privacy.

One Reed, an optical lens grinder, was the victim of a similar exploitation in an Indiana case decided in 1949, one year after the *Pallas* decision in Michigan. During World War II, Reed was attached to a mobile optical unit operating near the front lines in France. His picture was taken by the War Department for publication in the United States as part of a news item concerning overseas military activities and as part of a plan to bolster home front morale. Released by the Office of War Information, the picture appeared in publications, especially in Reed's home town. Defendant, a company back home that manufactured optical lenses, adopted the picture for use in connection with its own commercial enterprise. Reed brought action for invasion of his privacy and asked for damages to compensate him for the loss he had suffered, due to the fact that the previous use of the picture by the defendant now prevented its use for his own commercial purposes. The defendant contended that plaintiff had become a public personage upon entering the Army and had thereby lost his privacy. The court agreed that Reed had lost his privacy to the extent of any legitimate use the military authorities had seen fit to make of his person, but such extent did not include all of his privacy. A judgment of $20,000 in favor of the plaintiff was reduced on appeal to $1,000. The court reasoned that, while his privacy had been invaded, the larger award had been granted as compensation for the destruction of the value of a photograph to which he had no right. The negative belonged to the United States Army.

Another form of advertising is the form letter sent to prospective customers. Such a letter was sent out by a life insurance company after the employment of the person whose name and signature appeared in the letter had terminated. Action was brought for invasion of privacy. The Texas court had not been called upon before to decide the question of privacy, but it expressed the feeling that such right would be recognized in a proper case. The instant case was not deemed to be a proper one since, in the opinion of the court, no damages had been suffered by the plaintiff, nor was there any evidence to indicate that the defendant had gained by the use of plaintiff's name and signature. Later cases, which will be discussed in a subsequent chapter, show that the right of privacy is not recognized in Texas. It should also be noted that the United States Circuit Court of Appeals (fifth circuit) , in 1955, upheld a verdict of $1,200 awarded to a plaintiff whose picture was used in the advertisement of a business after her employment had terminated.

Speaking of insurance, an interesting case involving an insurance company was decided by the highest court of Louisiana in 1955. The plaintiff had been involved in an automobile accident, in which the driver of the other car was killed, and the plaintiff was so seriously injured that he was in no condition to supply any information. The defendant, plaintiff's insurance company, thought of a scheme whereby to acquire evidence, which it might use in defending against possible claims arisng out of the accident. An advertisement was inserted in a New Orleans newspaper, asking all persons who had witnessed the accident to contact the plaintiff. A New Orleans address and telephone number were included. The plea was addressed in the first person over the purported signature of the plaintiff. This was done without the plaintiff's knowledge or consent. As a matter of fact, the plaintiff was a resident of Baton Rouge and was engaged to a Baton Rouge girl. The address and telephone number given in the advertisement belonged to a female employee of the insurance company. Plaintiff's name was Hamilton, and, when the given telephone number was dialed, the person answering claimed to be Mrs. Hamilton. Some courts might say that the defendant was justified in choosing this method for the protection of its interests, that such was life, and that ordinary persons could take it. But the Louisiana court was sympathetic. Mr. Hamilton was awarded $5,000 for physical pain, suffering, and mental anguish; $2,500 for embarrassment and humiliation; and $5,000 for invasion of his privacy. We do not learn from the report of the case whether or not the insurance company eventually found its escapade worthwhile.

For our final case concerning invasion by advertising we go to Illinois, where the right of privacy was first recognized in 1952. An advertisement, designed to promote the sale of dog food, contained the photograph of a blind girl and depicted her as the prospective donee of a "Master Eye Dog." She was not in need of such a dog, since she already had one, nor had she consented to the use of her photograph. She brought action, claiming that her exposure in this manner had caused her to lose the respect and admiration of those who knew her, and to suffer humiliation and mental anguish. After pointing out that the question of privacy had never before been passed upon by an appellate court in Illinois, and after reviewing the status of privacy in other jurisdictions, the court concluded:

Basically, recognition of the right to privacy means that the law will take cognizance of an injury, even though no right of property or contract may be involved and even though the damages resulting are exclusively those of mental anguish. A person may not make an unauthorized appropriation of the personality of another, especially of his name or likeness, without being liable to him for mental distress as well as the actual pecuniary damages which the appropriation causes. The right of privacy is, of course, limited in cases of express or implied consent and in areas of legitimate public interest. But no such limitations are relevant in the instant case. Plaintiff was not a public figure, she did not consent to have the picture used, and there was no legitimate news interest in her likeness. Also, the right of privacy is sometimes limited to commercial situations. However, we need not discuss this limitation, because the instant case involves unauthorized advertising use of plaintiff's picture and would be comprehended within the narrowest definition of the right of privacy.

8

Invasion by Creditors

Strictly speaking, a creditor is a person to whom a debt is owed. Nevertheless, we shall group together, under the heading "Invasion by Creditors," the activities of creditors and the activities of those who claim to be creditors. Practically speaking, we can call a person a creditor if the debt he claims to be owing is not denied. Moreover, whether the debt be denied or not, the activities of which we shall speak are ordinarily carried on before any official establishment of the debt by a court of law. Hence, what we are concerned with is the question as to how far a creditor or claimant may go in seeking satisfaction without the aid of legal proceedings.

Legal proceedings are costly. It is, therefore, understandable that those whose claims are admitted, as well as those who conscientiously believe in the righteousness of their claims, should seek to obtain payment by all available means considered lawful. In their eagerness to avert the costs and hazards of litigation, some claimants so accelerate their efforts that the generated *momentum* causes them to traverse the outer limits of allowable activity. On the other hand, a claim asserted in error can cause embarrassment.

Take, for instance, the first and only privacy case to reach the highest court of Connecticut, *Urban v. Hartford Gas Co.* (1952). The plaintiff had bought a gas hot water heater from the defendant on the installment plan. One day, while the plaintiff was entertaining some guests, she was surprised by an unexpected visit. Employees of the gas company had come to remove the heater, claiming that the current installment had not been paid. Not only did the employees make known their business in the presence of the guests, but as a matter of fact the installment had been paid. The embarrassment would have been incisive enough even if the plaintiff had been delinquent, but to be subjected to embarrassment without the slightest provocation or the slimmest excuse is doubly painful. Plaintiff became hysterical and emotionally upset. An arrested diabetic condition flared up anew. Her prolonged illness was accompanied by great pain and mental anguish. She brought action for invasion of her privacy. The court did not commit itself as to the recognition of a right of privacy in

Connecticut, but concluded that, even if it were to hold that such right exists in Connecticut, there was no invasion of privacy involved in this case. The court made further comment that a possible recovery might be had on the ground of negligence, if it could be shown that the defendant could reasonably foresee the injury resulting from its conduct. It is difficult to agree that the exposure of plaintiff's private affairs, whether neglected or not, was not an invasion of her privacy. Surely discretion would have dictated forbearance to pursue the private matter in the presence of guests.

Back in 1927, a Kentucky court would not condone the exposure of a debtor to public notice. Perhaps it was because the method used by the creditor to pressure his debtor was so aggressive and so bizarre. The debtor was a veterinarian; the creditor, a proprietor of an automobile garage. A sign, five feet by eight feet, was placed in the show window of the garage:

Notice

Dr. W. R. Morgan owes an account here of $49.67. And if promises would pay an account this account would have been settled long ago. This account will be advertised as long as it remains unpaid.

Assuming the truth of the creditor's claim, Dr. Morgan had no cause of action on the ground of libel, since truth was a complete defense to an action of libel in Kentucky. However, the court held that what the creditor had done constituted an invasion of the right of privacy.

In Wisconsin it was a different story. There, in 1936, a debtor who claimed that his privacy had been invaded by the publication of his debt lost his case. The plaintiff, according to a statement of account held by the defendant, owed the latter $4.32 for goods sold and delivered. This account, together with twenty-three other accounts, was listed on handbills published by the defendant for the purpose of selling the accounts to the highest bidder. The court held that, until the legislature saw fit to create a right of privacy, there could be no action for invasion in Wisconsin.

Creditors are in a most advantageous position to exert pressure when their debtors happen to be employees. Employees are highly vulnerable to reflections cast upon their usefulness, efficiency, and qualifications, by the exposure of their indebtedness. Unless carefully protected by proper clauses in union contracts, or unless made firm by binding personal agreements, their tenure is subject to the whims of their employers. Indebtedness alone is not a justifiable cause for dismissal. Exposure of indebtedness may cause an employee to be singled out for special scrutiny, to which others, whose similar situations lie unexposed, are not subjected. The employer-employee relationship is far different from the master-servant relationship of yesteryear. No longer should the employer be looked upon as the practitioner of paternalistic control, nor should the personal affairs of the one be allowed to become the concern of the other. Shall we allow the creditor of an employee to interfere with the relationship, to jeopardize the employee's status, and to instill prejudice in the mind of the employer? Shall we allow the creditor to use the relationship as a weapon of destruction? The following cases give the answer.

The view taken in the State of Washington is found in *Lewis v. Physicians and Dentists Credit Bureau* (1947). The Credit Bureau had contacted the employer of Mrs. Lewis by telephone and advised him that she and her husband owed a bill, and that her wages would be garnished unless the bill was paid. When Mr. and Mrs. Lewis brought action for invasion of their privacy, the court found it unnecessary to align itself either for or against the recognition of a right of privacy. It felt that, even if it were to recognize such right, the conduct of the Credit Bureau in this case did not constitute a violation. Looking at the treatment of such cases in other jurisdictions, the court found that relief had been granted in cases of undue or oppressive publicity, as by conspicuous posting or publication in a newspaper. The court showed little sympathy for debtors when it said:

> People who do not pay their bills cannot object to some publicity in connection with attempts to collect them; their tender sensibilities are protected only from "undue or oppressive publicity."

Patton v. Jacobs (1948), an Indiana case, also involved the questionable conduct of a collection agency. The plaintiff was a female telephone operator working for the Veterans Administration. One defendant was a physician; the other was the Medical & Dental Business Bureau, Inc. to which the physician had turned over an account for collection. The Bureau sent letters to the Veterans Administration, asking for assistance in the collection of the bill. The Indiana court looked at other cases and came to the conclusion that debtors could complain only when creditors gave to the general public information concerning private matters in which the public had no legitimate interest, and when this was done in a manner that was coercive and oppressive. It is interesting to read what the court had to say about the interest of employers in the affairs of their employees:

> It must be borne in mind that an employer has a natural and proper interest in the facts relative to debts owed by his employees. He is subject

to the expense and inconvenience of defending himself in garnishee proceedings wherein a percentage of his employees' wages may be taken
to apply on such debts and thus additional and burdensome bookkeeping
entries may be imposed upon him. He has a right to hire only those who
pay their debts and may take a pardonable pride in the reputation of his
employees in that respect. He is not in a category with the general public
which cannot have any legitimate interest in a purely private matter between a creditor and a debtor. For the reasons above stated an employer
has a right to know the status of the financial obligations of his employees
and, while we cannot say that a creditor of an employee owes the employer a duty in that regard, it is difficult to follow a course of reasoning
that concludes that the employee's right of privacy has been invaded by
giving his employer information which the employer has a right to have.
In other words, an employee has no right of privacy as against his employer in the matter of the debts he owes and a creditor who gives such
information to the employer, unaccompanied by slanderous, libelous,
defamatory or coercive matter, incurs no liability in so doing. The fact
that in the usual course of business the communication may pass through
the hands of clerks or stenographers, whether in the employ of the writer
or the addressee, does not alter the rule. The situation is somewhat
analogous to that of a privileged communication which does not lose its
character through such process.

The court creates the illusion of full-dress participation of employers in garnishment proceedings. The only part played by the employer
is his compliance with a court order directing him to withhold from
the employee a percentage of his wages, just as he is now duty-bound
to do in the case of income and social security taxes. Considering the
multitudiness deductions now accomplished by employers, the original
groans having subsided, the burden added by a writ of garnishment is
negligble. Except for this, upon what further basis does an employer
have an interest in the financial responsibility of his employees? What
pride is his to take in the fact that his employees pay their debts? What
shame is his to bear when they become indebted? If his wage is fair,
his working conditions admirable, his product qualitatively sound, his
service reliable, how can the private affairs of his employees in any
way reflect upon his public relations?

The facts of a 1951 Kentucky case were similar, and the result was
the same, except that three judges dissented. The plaintiff was an
employee of the United States Government at the Louisville Medical
Depot. The defendant was in the employ of the Aetna Finance Company. A letter addressed by the defendant to the personnel director of
the Depot informed the latter that plaintiff had signed a $300 note as
surety for his cousin; that the cousin was unemployed; and that the
plaintiff refused to pay the $281.84 balance. The letter, in which a self-

addressed stamped envelope was enclosed, ended with this statement: "Anything you can do for us in this matter will certainly be appreciated." The slim majority of the Kentucky court, after reiterating the interest of employers in the ability and reputation of employees as to the payment of debts, held that the plaintiff had failed to state a cause of action. Two years later the Kentucky court turned down a similar request for relief, and again three judges dissented.

We should note that the employer involved in the Indiana case and in the 1951 Kentucky case was the United States Government. It is ironical that the courts should attribute to such an employer the interests which their judicial reasoning seems to conjoin with the rights of private employers.

Is it permisisble for a creditor to visit his debtor at the place where the latter is employed? In 1953, a Federal District Court in the western district of Oklahoma held that a creditor had the right to take reasonable steps to collect a delinquent debt. In that case, the facts showed that a bank held a chattel mortgage on a car which was brought, by the plaintiff, from Oklahoma to Texas and disposed of. An unpaid balance was still owed on the loan made by the bank to the plaintiff. A representative of the bank suddenly appeared at the place where the plaintiff was employed, while a police officer waited in a car outside. The representative asked for the plaintiff, she was called, and when she saw him she asked him to wait outside. She soon followed and was beckoned into the car in which the police officer was seated. Questioned about her account, she asked to be driven home where she claimed to have the chattel mortgage. The representative obliged. Once home, she dug out some papers and exhibited them. Although the case is not clear on the point, it seems safe to conclude that the chattel mortgage was not among the papers exhibited, for the court found as a matter of fact that the plaintiff was still indebted to the bank. Although the removal and disposition of the mortgaged car, as well as the presence of the police officer might suggest a justification of what transpired on criminal grounds, the court dealt with the case merely on the basis of a debtor-creditor relationship. When plaintiff complained that her privacy had been invaded, the court felt that the conduct of the defendant as a creditor was reasonable. It also pointed to the fact that defendant had caused no commotion, and that plaintiff had acted "of her own volition." The question remains as to whether or not the embarrassment caused by the defendant was justified. So far, we have found sympathy for employee-debtors only in dissenting opinions. Another example is given in the 1956 Michigan case that follows.

A collection agency addressed a letter to the assistant director of a junior college regarding a balance of $21.98 claimed to be owed by an employee of the college to a moving and storage company. The body of the letter reads as follows:

> Dear Sir:
>
> The above individual has been given every reasonable opportunity to pay or make satisfactory arrangements. Failure to do so justifies collection by legal action. This will, of course, bring additional expense upon your empoyee and inconvenience you as garnishee defendant. We would like to prevent both.
>
> We therefore suggest that you confer with this debtor to secure cooperation to that end. If the individual's resources will not permit payment in full, we suggest payroll deductions to provide assurance of regular remittance to this office. Payments of $5.00 or more per week are acceptable.
>
> Your help to avoid suit will be appreciated.

A majority of the Michigan court held that the sending of this letter did not constitute an invasion of privacy, but two judges dissented. The reasoning of the dissenters is shown in the following excerpt taken from the dissenting opinion:

> There is no need, in this opinion, to undertake a lengthy exposition of the right of privacy, of the growth of the law from those ancient days when only a physical battery found redress in the courts, when gross and evil assaults upon the spirits and emotions of our people went without recovery. That the right of privacy exists in this jurisdiction was settled beyond doubt by the case of Pallas v. Crowley, Milner & Co. . . . It involves not only the right against appropriation of some elements of plaintiff's personality for commerical use, the Pallas case, but also the right against the disclosure of private information concerning the private life of a private citizen in violation of the common decencies, such as the publication of a picture of one's deformed child . . ., the details of an humiliating illness . . ., or the fact that he has not paid his debts. . . . The common denominator in all of these cases is an unreasonable and serious interference with the plaintiff's interest in not having his affairs known to others. The wrong depends not on conduct otherwise tortious (i.e., trespass, defamation) nor does it turn upon breach of confidence, or truth or untruths, or an arithmetical measure of the numbers who witnessed the exposure, or the particular method thereof, whether by placard, or by letter. The wrong is done when the curtain of privacy is lifted.

According to the dissenters, all that creditors should be allowed to do is request payment, demand payment, sue, and garnish.

What happened in Ohio left no doubt in the minds of the judges that constituted the highest court in that state as to how they should rule on the question of recognizing the right of privacy and on the question of invasion involved in the case brought before them in 1956. That case, like others discussed above, dealt with the conduct of a collection agency. The plaintiff was a school teacher who was indebted to a doctor. The court found that the agency had initiated a campaign designed to harrass and torment the debtor: by telephoning the debtor six or eight times every day, at home and at his place of employment, sometimes as late as 11:45 P.M., over a period of three weeks; by telephoning the superiors of the debtor and informing them of the debt; and by telephoning the debtor at his place of employment three times within fifteen minutes, with the result that a loss of employment was threatened. All this, felt the court, was unreasonable and amounted to an invasion of privacy.

Must conduct be almost unimaginably outrageous before it is considered as constituting an invasion? As we have already seen, some courts are fearful that a liberal acceptance and application of privacy doctrines will lead to abuse by potential claimants. An example of such abuse may be found in a Kentucky case decided in 1956. In that case, the plaintiff claimed that his privacy had been invaded when his landlord came on a Sunday morning to collect the rent. Perhaps some would sympathize with the sentiments of the plaintiff, but it seems that most people would agree with the court that the claim was a bit far fetched. However, this situation is quite different from those in which it seems that whatever abuse has been practiced can be attributed to the crafty methods employed by some creditors.

9

Invasion by Magazines, Newspapers, and Books

The written page may serve various purposes. It may be used for dissemination of information of an educational nature. It may be used to provide amusement. It may be used for advocacy of a cause. It may be used to satisfy idle curiosity. It may be used as a vehicle for bestowing honor. It may be used to besmirch a reputation. It may be used for the promotion of public welfare. It may be used to advance the monetary aims of the writer.

To seek wealth is perfectly proper, but care must be taken that such pursuit be not accomplished by unlawful means. As slavery is outlawed, so too should all unauthorized uses of personality for private gain be outlawed. The Constitutional guarantee of a free press must not be allowed to serve as a cloak of protection against liability for unwarranted exploitations of personality. Such guarantee was originally conceived as a safeguard against governmental abuses of power. In a broad sense, it serves to protect and promote the public interest involved in past and current events.

It seems that an aggrieved individual must bow to the superior interest of the public in matters involving the interests of both. Black's *Law Dictionary* has this, among other things, to say about public interest:

> Something in which the public, the community at large, has some pecuniary interest, or some interest by which their legal rights or liabilities are affected. It does not mean anything so narrow as mere curiosity, or as the interests of the particular localities, which may be affected by the matters in question.

The important thing to note is that public curiosity is not public interest. He who seeks to satisfy idle curiosity seeks only to amuse, and no provider of amusement should be allowed to use unwilling human beings as his "props."

Magazines

While some magazines may be classed as primarily informative, others

are aimed at meeting the demand for amusement, and still others perform a dual function. Some are presented in the plainest of forms
while others are adorned with illustrations and attractive covers. If
the purpose be a noble one, the design to attract cannot be seized upon
as a ground for complaint. But if attractiveness is accomplished through
exploitations of personality, nobility of purpose should not be accepted
as justification. And if the matter under discussion be one in which
the public has a legitimate interest, it is not always necessary or proper
to focus attention upon an individual whose circumstances may place
him within the orbit of the discourse.

The following item was published in a weekly news magazine on
the page entitled "Medicine:"

Starving Glutton

One night last week pretty Mrs. ———— of Kansas City grabbed a candy
bar, packed up some clothes, and walked to General Hospital. "I want
to stay here," she said between bites. "I want to eat all the time. I can
finish a normal meal and be back in the kitchen in ten minutes eating
again."

Dr. ———— immediately packed her off to a ward, ordered a big meal
from

> [Here was inserted a picture of the patient, showing her lying
> in bed and wearing a long-sleeve hospital gown; a close-up
> showing only her face, head and arms, with bedclothes over
> her chest; under the picture, "Insatiable-Eater . . . . She
> eats for ten."]

the hospital kitchen while he questioned Mrs. ————. He found that
although she had eaten enough in the past year to feed a family of ten,
she had lost 25 pounds. After a preliminary examination Dr. ————
thought that Mrs. ———'s pancreas might be functioning abnormally, that
it might be burning up too much sugar in her blood and somehow causing excessive flow of digestive juices, which sharpened her appetite.

While he made painstaking laboratory tests and discussed advisability
of a rare operation, Mrs. ——— lay in bed and ate.

Did the publication of this article, including its pictorial illustration,
constitute an invasion of privacy? This question was decided in the
affirmative by the highest court of Missouri in 1942. The court observed
that "establishing conditions of liability for invasion of the right of
privacy is a matter of harmonizing individual rights with community
and social interests." After noting that the plaintiff had protested
against publictiy, and that her picture was taken by one reporter while
another was engaged in attempting to persuade her to consent, the court
concluded:

> Certainly if there is any right of privacy at all, it should include the right to obtain medical treatment at home or in a hospital for an individual personal condition (at least if it is not contagious or dangerous to others) without personal publicity . . . . It was not necessary to state plaintiff's name in or to give medical information to the public as to the symptoms, nature, causes or results of her ailment . . . . Certainly plaintiff's picture conveyed no medical information. While plaintiff's ailment may have been a matter of some public interest because unusual, certainly the identity of the person who suffered this ailment was not.

The foregoing case involved a highly reputable magazine, as did also the following case, decided by the Federal District Court in the District of Columbia in 1948. The latter case arose as the result of an article entitled "Never Give a Passenger a Break." The article was a satire on taxi-cab drivers in Washington. A female taxi-cab driver found her photograph among the illustrations used in the article. To the extent that the satire might be found to have cast aspersions upon her, the plaintiff claimed it to be libelous; to the extent that she was singled out without her consent, she claimed it to be an invasion of her privacy. The court agreed. As to the matter of privacy, the court held that any publication of a person's photograph without his sanction was a violation of the privacy right, unless the person, by reason of position or achievement, had become a public character.

What is a public character? Black's *Law Dictionary* says: "Public character. An individual who asks for and desires public recognition, such as a statesman, author, artist, or inventor." How do we classify the unassuming hero, the criminal, the unfortunate victim? And if a person is a public character, is he subject to unrestrained exploitation? If a person has been photographed in connection with a public matter, may the photograph be used indiscriminately in association with publications having nothing to do with the photograph? The Pennsylvania view on this subject may be gathered from the opinion expressed in the case that follows.

Another issue of the magazine that had carried the article on taxi-cab drivers included an article entitled "Crime Was My Business." The article consisted of an account of the experiences of a former California police chief. Placed within the confines of the article was a photograph, taken by a newspaperman some three years before, showing three police officers and a robbery suspect. The candid shot portrayed the suspect, who had been caught by two of the officers, lunging forward toward the floor and being grabbed by the three uniformed men. The article gave no explanation of a possible connection between the scene por-

trayed and the experiences being recounted. The photograph had
been bought from a news agency in New York. It was selected from
seventy-five offerings as most suitable to the purpose of illustrating the
article. Beneath the photograph were the following words: "One of
the compensations in a policeman's life is the thrill he gets out of
walking into a potentially dangerous situation and knowing that it is
his presence there that brings order. 'If I had to do it all over again,'
says Mr. Powers, 'I'd still be a cop'." Mr. Powers was the police chief
whose experiences were the subject matter of the article. Presumably,
the three policemen in the picture had no connection with Mr. Powers.
They complained that their portrayal had caused some people to look
upon them as bullies, and that in any case their portrayal under the
circumstances was an invasion of their privacy. The case was decided
in 1956, and the court had little trouble in reaching its decision. It
so happened that, according to the Statute of Limitations, actions for
invasion of privacy had to be commenced within two years after their
accrual. Despite the fact that this action was brought too late, the
court indicated its feeling that a timely action would not have produced a more favorable result for, in its opinion, the privacy of the
three police officers had not been invaded.

In the same year, a Federal court in Pennsylvania decided another
case involving the republication in a magazine of a picture originally
published in a newspaper. A man had been kicked to death by the
leader of a teen-age gang. During the ensuing period of public commotion, his widow consented to a newspaper photographer's request that
she pose with her six minor children. Two Pittsburgh papers published
the picture and the story. The picture was made available to the Associated Press, that made it available to World Wide Photos, Inc., that
made it available to a detective story magazine, that republished the
picture and story three months later under the title "Heartbreak
House." It was this publication in a magazine published primarily
for amusement that led the widow to bring action, on her own behalf
and on behalf of her children. There was no question in the mind of
the court as to the principal purpose of the magazine:

> We assume, as plaintiffs contend, that the magazine *Front Page Detec-
> tive* is published principally for entertaining purposes and is not pri-
> marily intended to inform the reading public. . . .

On the other hand, the court felt that the inclusion of the three-
month-old story and picture in a magazine designed principally for
entertainment was justified. Why? Because:

In addition to being newsworthy, the plaintiffs, through the widow, agreed that the pictures of the family should be a part of the news; they consented to become actors in an occurrence of public interest; they voluntarily attached themselves pictorially to this news item. It is true that plaintiffs did not consent to republication of this particular family picture by defendant three months later, but the privilege to publish pictures in connection with news is not lost after this lapse of time.

This is not like the cases of public figures whose pictures are exploited without their consent, in moving pictures or in advertisements. Neither is it like the cases where newsworthy events and accompanying pictures are distorted, fictionized, garnished, ridiculed or falsified in a republication.

What is news? The term itself connotes freshness. Certainly events of the past cannot be considered news. How then can a publication which delves into the past be justified on the basis of newsworthiness? Was *Front Page Detective* bent on publishing news when it republished the picture of a widow and her minor children three months after the occurrence that gave rise to the picture? Let us look at what another Federal court in Pennslvania had to say about a questionable publication five years earlier.

When the plaintiff was eleven or twelve, a magazine published by the defendant contained a photograph, taken two years before, showing the plaintiff as she lay in the street immediately following an accident. Her face was distorted by pain and terror, her hair disheveled, her clothing disarranged, and her legs exposed to the hips. The defendant contended that the picture was unusual, striking and dramatic; that the picture was of such superlative merit that, as a photograph, it was entitled to publication without the consent of its subject. The plaintiff contended that the photograph fell into the category of sensationalism. The court found in favor of the plaintiff. The basis of its opinion lay in its contrived distinction between an event considered newsworthy and one not deserving such designation; although fine indeed, and of questionable import, it settled the issue:

> . . . But the courts are not concerned with the canons of good taste, and pictures which startle, shock, and even horrify may be freely published, provided they are not libelous or indecent, if the subject of the picture consents or if the occasion is such that his right of privacy does not protect him from the publication. The right is, of course, variable and in some cases it may dwindle almost to the vanishing point, as where an individual, perhaps involuntarily, becomes involved in some newsworthy event or some situation in which the public has a legitimate interest. In the present case the subject of the picture was a trivial traffic accident. The girl was not hurt, the motorist was fined for running through a red

light . . . . and that was all there was to it. It is not pretended that the picture had the slightest news value when the defendant got hold of it and published it two years after the event.

The tenor of the foregoing statement would seem to indicate that the court did not think that the event was newsworthy even at its inception, let alone two years later. But the court had even more to say in denouncing the sort of photographic publication that is altogether too common:

> . . . But I do not think that a private individual waives anything merely because he goes on the public street. Perhaps he cannot complain if someone snaps his picture without asking permission, but publishing it is an entirely different matter.
>
> The sum of it seems to be that where a magazine chooses to publish, without permission, a picture of a private individual in a humiliating situation, for the sole purpose of attracting attention to a leading article, it takes the risk that a jury will find, as the jury in this case did, that the publisher should have realized that the publication would be offensive to a person of ordinary sensibilities and unreasonably interfere with her right of privacy.

While some are unintentionally caught in a situation when wide publication may cause embarrassment, others calculate a limited risk by inadvertently producing scenes that attract attention. Imagine a husband and wife during a lull in their business of running a confectionery and ice cream concession at the Farmers Market in Los Angeles. They chance to seat themselves in places ordinarily occupied by customers and to engage in an affectionate pose. Unknown to them, the sharp eye of a camera records the scene. The picture is published in the October, 1947, issue of *Harper's Bazaar* to illustrate an article entitled "And So the World Goes Round." Some years later, apparently when the couple was apprised of the publicity accorded to them, action was brought against the publisher. When they found that the Statute of Limitations had barred their action, they amended their complaint, alleging that the same picture had been republished, with defendant's consent, in the May, 1949, issue of the *Ladies' Home Journal,* a periodical put out by another publisher. The republication was in connection with an article called "Love," which discussed various types of love. Love consisting "wholly of sexual attraction and nothing else" was described as the "wrong kind of love." This type was attributed to the plaintiffs, beneath whose picture appeared the following: "Publicized as glamorous, desirable, 'love at first sight' is a bad risk." When action was brought against the publisher of the *Ladies' Home Journal,*

the court held that, if proved, the allegations showed an unwarranted
and unreasonable interference with plaintiffs' interest in not having
their likenesses exhibited to the public in this manner. Concerning
the complaint against the publisher of *Harper's Bazaar*, the court held
that consent to the republication of the picture in the *Ladies' Home
Journal* constituted no cause of action, unless it could also be shown
that the publisher likewise consented to the article accompanying the
republication.

Why was it necessary for the plaintiffs to show more than that the
publisher had consented to the republication? Was not the publication
of the picture itself an invasion of privacy? One dissenting judge
thought so, but the majority felt the publication only made it possible
for others to see what the plaintiffs had already made visible to those
in their immediate vicinity. Besides, thought the court, there was nothing uncomplimentary about the picture that would give the publisher
any reason to believe that its publication would offend persons of ordinary sensibilities. The court likened this exposure to pictures taken
of persons appearing in a parade, concluding that such would be impossible if people had the right, under all circumstances, to prevent
the publication of photographs taken without permission.

Was it fair to compare the scene in which the plaintiffs appeared
with the spectacle of a parade? And if there were anything uncomplimentary about the picture, would it not then fall within the realm
of libel rather than privacy? And what about purpose? Does not the
California court distinguish, as others do, between information and
entertainment? Apparently not:

> . . . Apparently the picture has no particular news value but is designed
> to serve the function of entertainment as a matter of legitimate public in-
> terest. . . . . However, the constitutional guarantees of freedom of ex-
> pression apply with equal force to the publication whether it be a news
> report or an entertainment feature, ... and defendants' liability ac-
> crues only in the event that it can be said that there has been a wrongful
> invasion of plaintiff's right of privacy.

Thus, purpose is no criterion in California. Invasion of privacy is
recognized if a publication is both unprivileged and offensive to ordinary sensibilities. That the publication is unprivileged is not enough,
as an erstwhile hero found out in 1954.

One day, in 1952, a woman thought of commiting suicide. In preparation for her plunge, she had climbed over the side of San Francisco's
Golden Gate Bridge. A man approached and made a vain attempt
to change her mind. A reporter caught the scene with his camera, and

the picture appeared in a San Francisco newspaper. Two years later, an article on suicides appeared in the *Saturday Evening Post,* and the same picture was used in connection therewith. Action was brought for invasion of privacy. The court found that the article did not refer to the picture, that the picture was not necessary to the article, and that it was used merely to illustrate a type of suicide. Considering the fact that the only purpose for which the photograph was used was to enhance the attractiveness of the magazine, was there an invasion of privacy? Not according to this court's view of privacy:

> An invasion of the right of privacy occurs not with the mere publication of a photograph, but occurs when a photograph is published where the publisher should have known that its publication would offend the sensibilities of a normal person, and whether there has been such an offensive invasion of privacy is to some extent a question of law. . . . Where the photograph portrays nothing to shock the ordinary sense of decency or propriety, where there is nothing uncomplimentary or discreditable in the photograph itself, and where the caption and article add nothing that makes the photograph uncomplimentary or discreditable no actionable invasion of the right of privacy occurs. . . .

It may thus be seen that, in California, a person cannot recover for invasion of privacy unless he can show (1) an unprivileged use of his personality, and (2) such use as would offend the sensibilities of a normal person. Where the public has no legitimate interest in the portrayal of a person such portrayal is unprivileged, but unless the unprivileged publication affects the feelings of the person portrayed there can be no recovery. What the California judiciary seems to overlook is the fact that a person may be as mentally affected by commercialization of his personality as by "uncomplimentary or discreditable" portrayals. On the other hand, why should not commercialization alone, even with no resulting mental effect, be considered an invasion of privacy? For some reason, the idea of associating invasion of privacy with injury to feelings, to the exclusion of any other conception, has taken so firm a hold in some jurisdictions that the professed recognition of the right of privacy seems to be lacking in substance.

Take the case of an automobile stunt driver whose brush with the law was fictionalized in the magazine called *Startling Detective.* Although responsible for the death of another, his indictment and trial for murder resulted in acquittal. The story provided attractive material for publishers of detective magazines. One such publisher seized the opportunity and dressed up the story for presentation in a fictionalized version. A Federal court in Connecticut was called upon, in 1935, to decide whether or not the stunt driver had a case.

Where an action for invasion of privacy, based upon a multi-state publication, is commenced in a Federal court, the law of the state wherein the plaintiff is domiciled governs, for the essence of the action is considered to be mental distress, which in turn is considered to be located at the domicile of the aggrieved party. The stunt driver was domiciled in Oklahoma, so Oklahoma law governed the case. But Oklahoma had not yet passed on the right of privacy. The Federal court in Connecticut felt sure that, when called upon, the Oklahoma court would follow the trend set in other jurisdictions and announce its recognition of the right as part of Oklahoma's common law.

Applying the same tests as had been laid down by the California court, the Federal court first looked to see whether or not the publication in question was privileged. Assuming the stunt driver to be a public figure, and that the public had an interest in public figures, a factual account would have been privileged, but the same could not be said of a fictionalized account. Said the court:

> To the extent that the defendant indulged in fictionalization, the inference gathers strength that the dominant characteristic of the story was not genuine information but fictional readability conducive to increased circulation for the magazine.

In other words, commercial exploitation of a story is not privileged. But in order that he be entitled to recovery the plaintiff had to allege and prove that his mental sensibilities had been seriously hurt by the story. Said the court:

> The right is not one that entitles a person to recover damages as a windfall in the absence of resulting hurt to his sensibilities.

Newspapers

We regard the primary function of a newspaper to be the dissemination of news. The public interest in newsworthy occurrences is beyond question. However, not all occurrences are newsworthy, nor all accounts and portrayals entirely proper or in good taste. As pointed out before, there is a vast difference between public interest and public curiosity. The public is entitled to information vital to the preservation and promotion of its rights and privileges. The public is not entitled to a view of private affairs in which it has no legitimate interest. The eagerness to sell newspapers too often causes publishers to become oblivious to their primary responsibilities. The getting of a story seems to be more important than the regard for individual rights. A picture used to be worth ten thousand words; today it is worth ten thousand dollars.

If a person is arrested and indicted for having allegedly committed a crime, is it necessary or proper that a newspaper report of the matter include a photograph portraying not only the alleged criminal but also the members of his family? Back in 1911, the highest court in the State of Washington decided that, whatever wrong had been done to one whose image was so portrayed along with that of the alleged criminal, such wrong did not fall within the rules theretofore recognized as permitting a recovery for invasion of the right of privacy.

The Supreme Judicial Court of Massachusetts has never ruled in favor of any plaintiff in actions for invasion of privacy. Its first opportunity arose in 1933. The case was a bit involved. The action was brought by a woman following the publication of a picture in connection with her suit for divorce, her husband's cross suit, and her husband's action against their chauffeur for alienation of affections. A group picture had been taken of plaintiff, her husband, the chauffeur, a pilot, and another person, in front of an airplane. When the picture appeared in a newspaper, all portions except the part in which plaintiff and the chauffeur could be seen, side by side, were somehow obliterated. The court held that plaintiff had stated a case of libel, but that she had failed to state a cause of action based upon the right of privacy. In support of its decision, the court made the following points: that plaintiff had voluntarily posed for the picture; that the picture had been taken at a public place; that plaintiff had no property right in the picture, and hence no right to prevent its publication; and that the circumstances imposed no express or implied limitations on the publication of the picture by the person owning it.

Considering the fact that only a portion of the original picture was published, can we not treat that portion separately and seriously question the conclusions expressed by the court? Did the plaintiff voluntarily pose for a picture to be taken of her and the chauffeur alone? If there was an expressed or implied consent to the publication of the original, could any such consent be implied as to the portion actually published? The plaintiff pressed this point, but the court replied:

> That contention cannot be supported. The question before us is strictly confined to this point. It does not relate to violations of privacy which would involve acts in the nature of nuisance, or which are appropriation of the photographic reproduction for purposes of advertisement. Questions of that nature may be dealt with when they arise.

Thus, the Massachusetts court, if it were to recognize the right of privacy, would confine its view to "acts in the nature of nuisance" and to uses "for purposes of advertisement." What is a nuisance? Blackstone described it as "anything that unlawfully worketh hurt, inconvenience, or damage." Surely the crafty manipulation of a photograph could hurt the feelings of persons affected and be classified as an act "in the nature of nuisance."

Another case involving the publication of a photograph in a newspaper was decided by the Massachusetts court in 1940. The picture showed the plaintiff in conversation with a police captain. Since the publication was justified if it concerned a matter of legitimate public interest, and since the complaint was silent as to the occasion for the publication, the court found that it was unnecessary to decide whether or not any right of privacy was recognized in the Commonwealth of Massachusetts. However, in the course of its opinion, the court went into a discussion as to the distinction between right of privacy and libel:

> The fundamental difference between a right to privacy and a right to freedom from defamation is that the former directly concerns one's own peace of mind, while the latter concerns primarily one's reputation, although the damages may take into account mental suffering. . . . Another important difference is that truth could not justify an invasion of a legally recognized right of privacy, although ordinarily truth is a defense to libel.

To illustrate the difference, the court referred to a previous libel case, in which the complaint was based upon a gossip column suggestion that a certain husband and his wife were unhappy. If the suggestion was untrue, a case of libel was established. "But even if true," observed the court, "that suggestion was an outrageous invasion of privacy, from the standpoint of decency, if not from that of law." According to this reasoning, Massachusetts would be willing to recognize an invasion of privacy but, in its estimation, a proper case has not yet arisen within that jurisdiction.

If the proper case arises, are we sure that justice will prevail? Take, for example, *Flake v. Greensboro News Co.,* a case decided in North Carolina in 1938. The plaintiff was a radio entertainer (a female singer) who, in bathing attire, had posed for a publicity picture taken in a CBS studio. The picture was inserted by mistake in a newspaper advertisement concerned with the sale of bread and the promotion of a theater attraction called *Folies de Paree.* Where the image of Sally Paine, star of the show, should have appeared, that of the plaintiff appeared in its place. Disturbed by the fact that she had been portrayed in connection with what she termed a "cheap sexy show," Miss Flake brought action for libel and invasion of privacy.

Now to establish a case of libel, one must show that he has been portrayed in such manner that the portrayal itself is libelous, as when one is portrayed as a thief, or that the portrayal, given its full import by the surrounding circumstances, has caused substantial damage to his reputation. The court found that plaintiff's portrayal as the star of *Folies de Paree* was not in itself debasing, nor was it satisfied that any resulting damage had been shown.

But what of privacy? Had it not been invaded? Oh yes! The court's reasoning led to that conclusion:

> So far as we have been able to ascertain, no court has yet held that it constitutes a tort for a newspaper to publish an image of an individual when such publication is not libelous, except when such publication involves the breach of a trust, the violation of a contract, or when the photograph is used in connection with some commercial enterprise, and we are presently called upon to decide only the right of an individual to prohibit the unauthorized use of an image of her features and figure in connection with and as part of an advertisement.

So plaintiff had a case. But what did the invasion cost the defendant? The court put it this way:

> We are of the opinion that the reasoning in the Pavesich case, supra, is sound and establishes the correctness of the conclusion that the unauthorized use of one's photograph in connection with an advertisement or other commercial enterprise gives rise to a cause of action which would entitle the plaintiff, without the allegation and proof of special damages, to a judgment for nominal damages, and to injunctive relief, if and when the wrong is persisted in by the offending parties.

While the North Carolina court agreed with the reasoning of the Georgia court in the Pavesich case, it did not entirely follow the Georgia conception. The Georgia court was willing to allow damages for injuries to feelings, without proof of special damages. The North Carolina court limited its allowance to nominal damages, damages in name only, a mere token of victory without substance. Said the court:

> The law seeks to compensate for damages to the person, the reputation, or the property of an individual. It cannot and does not undertake to compensate for mere hurt or embarrassment alone.

It is difficult to think of a court recognizing privacy upon a purely commercial basis and then denying compensatory damages to the victim of an invasion. Models are paid for the services they render to advertising agencies. Why should not a person who has, without authority, been placed in a similar position be entitled to reasonable compensation?

Perhaps some would say that we are dealing here with minutiae. Apathy and complacency all too often produce expressions that minimize the full impact of a wrong. Too often is emphasis placed upon attempts to justify wrongs, while the plights of victims are reduced to ashes. The culprit becomes a hero, while the injured party is portrayed as a Shylock seeking his pound of flesh. In the name of freedom, clothed in the robes of public interest, newspaper sensationalists pry open the lid of privacy and nurture the hunger of curiosity. To struggle for freedom only to be devoured by it makes little sense. To headline domestic breaches reduces the chances of reconciliation and defeats the aim of preserving the marital relationship. While fear of publicity may work as a deterrent, it is more likely to suppress the innocent party by its coercive force than to deter the blameworthy party whose conscience is impregnable. And if there is a public interest in domestic relations, must the private principals involved be converted into public figures?

There are times when a person finds himself in an unfortunate position, having all he can do to cope with his predicament without being bothered by newspapermen seeking to produce and to dramatize a story. Parties to domestic relations proceedings may be looked upon as occupying such an uncoveted position. Let us look in on a domestic relations proceeding that led to an action for invasion of privacy.

A man had obtained an uncontested divorce and the custody of two minor children. The former wife later petitioned for an order setting aside the decree, claiming that her former husband had threatened her with bodily harm and injury to her reputation if she contested. Her petition was granted, and new divorce proceedings were ordered. An appeal from this order was pending when the question of custody came up for hearing. The parties were in court, and so were the children. The father contended that the mother was not fit to have custody of the children, and he had witnesses to substantiate his contention. During a recess in the proceedings, a newspaper photographer entered the courtroom and, over the protests of the male principal, snapped pictures of him. A newspaper calling itself *The Picture Newspaper* carried the pictures and the story. Action for invasion of privacy was commenced in the Federal District Court of Minnesota. The complaint was so eloquently drawn, it would take great restraint to resist the temptation to quote portions of it here. It recited that the plaintiff:

> . . . did lead a quiet peaceful life free from the prying curiosity and un-
> mitigated gossip which accompanies fame, notoriety, and scandal; . . .
> did pursue his useful toil with its homely joys and destiny obscure, did
> deem it wise and provident and comforting to keep the noiseless tenor of
> his way far from the maddening crowd's ignoble strife of scandal and no-
> toriety; . . . . has ever shunned and avoided notoriety and publicity, and
> has ever held as precious his right of privacy relative to his personality,
> his acts, sayings, and pictures, in all his social relations, his church groups,
> and his business transactions.

It further stated that plaintiff "has never exhibited himself, nor exploited his family life, his reputation, or his picture for money, profit,
or commercial gain." It alleged that the defendants

> . . . with deliberate intent, . . . and being specifically advised that they were
> forbidden to take, use, and publish in any shape, form, or posture the
> pictures of the plaintiff, did [while plaintiff was in the courtroom] willfully
> and maliciously, with intent to injure this plaintiff and bring him into
> public notoriety and to destroy the comfort of his life, and also the peace
> and tranquility of his mind, and to thrust upon this plaintiff unsought,
> unwarranted, and undesired publicity and notoriety utterly obnoxious
> to the plaintiff and with intent to annihilate and destroy the seclusion of
> plaintiff's private life, and to exploit plaintiff's name and personality,
> did willfully, wantonly, and maliciously take said plaintiff's picture . . .
> over and above the express protests of the plaintiff and his legal counsel,
> and did publish the said plaintiff's picture in the said *Times,* The Pic-
> ture Paper," . . . together with certain comments thereon, over and above
> his express objections and expressions of disapproval.

The plaintiff also alleged that he had suffered damage; that his personality had been violated and cheapened; that he had been made notori-
ous; that he had become subject to contempt, ridicule, and the inquisi-
tive notice of the general public; that the publication had outraged
the finer sentiments of his nature, humiliated his self-respect, destroyed
his peace of mind, violated his privacy, and caused him to suffer great
mental pain, anguish, humiliation and distress.

After observing that Minnesota had no privacy statute, and that
the right of privacy had never before been passed upon in Minnesota,
the court found it unnecessary to pass upon that question for, in its
opinion, the plaintiff had no right to recovery anyway. Said the court:

> Certainly, this Court should proceed with caution before it attempts to
> sit as a censor and to interfere with the traditional right of the Press to
> print all printable news which appears in the public records of our courts.
> Unfortunate as it may be for the principals who make charges and defend
> counter-charges of misconduct in order to obtain freedom from an al-
> legedly erring spouse or the custody of their children in divorce pro-

ceedings, the indisputable fact remains that there are many people in the immediate community where the action is pending who look to the Press for all such details, and it does not seem to avail that the more intelligent public deprecates that such published details "usurp the place of interest in brains capable of other things." p. 196, 4 H.L.R.

Moreover, it cannot be controverted that there is a wide-spread interest in this very kind of news and perhaps it is not strange that it should be so. Most people are interested in the weather because it generally concerns all classes of people. Domestic disputes, controversies between parents and others as to the custody of minor children, allowances of alimony, and the various acts and conduct recognized by the courts as grounds for divorce, are probably of interest to a large number of people because in their own immediate lives to a greater or less degree, such problems have concerned their friends and acquaintances and sometimes their own immediate families. And as recognized by the eminent writers from whom the doctrine of the right of privacy stems, "it is only the more flagrant breaches of decency and propriety that could in practice be reached, and it is not perhaps desirable even to attempt to repress everything which the nicest taste and keenest sense of the respect due to private life would condemn." p. 216, 4 H.L.R.

No one complains about the publication of weather reports, but he who is singled out and subjected to the scrutiny of idle curiosity merits consideration. The law should rather restrain than encourage infringements upon the dignity of individuals. Let a man have his day in court without the piercing eyes of notoriety.

If a man has had his day in court and comes forth only with the scars of battle, shall these be reopened by the pointed pen of the press? There was a man who was arrested when slot machines were found on his property. He was charged with having set up and maintained gambling devices in violation of the law. His trial resulted in an acquittal. Six months later, a newspaper article described police efforts to eradicate gambling activities in counties adjacent to Bucks County, Pennsylvania. In the course of the article, reference was made to the fact that it was six months since slot machines had been exposed in Bucks County, when they had been found on the property of the person named. When he brought action against the newspaper publisher, for libel and invasion of privacy, the plaintiff got little sympathy from the court. As for the libel, the court reasoned that plaintiff's reputation had not been injured for, while he had been acquitted of having set up and maintained gambling devices, he could have been tried for possession of such devices. This reasoning is difficult to digest, in view of the totality of implications which might be drawn from the story. Even if such implications were confined to the element of possession alone, would the truth of the past justify an impingement upon a present reputation? As for the invasion of privacy, the court found that the newspaper story afforded plaintiff no basis for complaint. This 1954 decision in Pennsylvania is not unusual; it further demonstrates a careless regard for the sanctity of privacy and the dignity of personality.

Another demonstration of the same may be found in a 1954 decision handed down by the United States Circuit Court of Appeals sitting in Texas. Let the court tell the story:

> On January 22, 1951, appellant, a dancing instructor, received a minor injury while riding as a passenger in a bus of the Houston Transit Company. Subsequently, she filed suit for personal injuries against said company, and the next day the *Houston Chronicle,* a daily newspaper with a wide circulation, carried on page one of its Sunday edition a story concerning the suit, along with a cartoon or caricature depicting the plaintiff dancing with an animated bus. The headlines of the column read as follows: "Asks $132,500 for 'Unreasonable Jerk.' Bus Skips, Dancer Flips, Suit Nips." Appellant also complains of the following phraseology in the article: "A Houston Transit Company bus that did the boomps-a-daisy when it should have been doing a smooth waltz caused a 45-year-old English dancing teacher to file a $132,500 damage suit in federal court Saturday. The lady claimed she did a very ungraceful adagio flip half way up the aisle of a jerky bus . . . .

The dancing teacher brought action for libel and invasion of privacy. Texas law was applicable to the case. Under that law, in order to succeed in an action of libel, one would have to establish defamation tending to injure or impeach his reputation. Since the plaintiff alleged only that she had been held up to ridicule, her libel action failed. That she had been flagrantly held up to ridicule could not be doubted. And if her libel action had to fail, surely she could rely on a recognition of her injury on another ground! Does not the right of privacy encompass what has been called the inviolate personality? But, as the court observed, no right of privacy action has as yet been recognized in the State of Texas.

South Carolina professes to recognize the right of privacy, but its highest court has yet to uphold a claim of invasion. In 1956, it was held that no cause of action had been stated on the basis of the following newspaper article:

> A chubby, blonde 12-year-old mother of a day-old healthy baby boy greeted visitors cheerfully yesterday, but declined to have her picture taken or talk generally with reporters.
> Her young husband, ————, a West Columbia construction company

worker whose age could not be learned, also declined to see newsmen or let his wife talk with outsiders after an Associated Press reporter talked to her briefly.

Mrs. ———, in the brief visit she granted the news service reporter, was cheerful but uncommunicative.

She had just concluded a nursing visit from her young son. At her orders, the baby was placed in the obstetrical ward nursery at a point where he cannot be seen by outsiders through the viewing window.

.   .   .   .

Occupying a choice private room, she would say only that she had read *The State* lying in her bed.

I just don't want any publicity," she said pleasantly. She agreed to reconsider the matter in a later talk with her husband, but both stood by her original decision, hospital attendants said.

The hospital said the six-pound, 14-ounce baby was "fine and healthy." He was seen as he was carried by a nurse from the room to the nursery and his appearance bore out the hospital judgment.

Mrs. ———'s family—her father is listed as ——— ——— from Georgia, but from what place could not be learned.

We are so used to publicity of this sort that it seems almost hopeless to expect a calloused public to appreciate the deep significance of such treatment. The article itself is replete with the yearning for privacy, and yet the pleas of those concerned have gone unheeded. The court was proud to announce that the right of privacy was recognized in South Carolina, and the previous decision upon which this announcement was based had proclaimed the right of privacy as a right to live without publicity. Why then was relief denied in this case? Because, after weighing the conflicting interests involved, the court felt compelled to decide against the complainant. First, the problem was presented:

> The right of privacy is not an absolute right. Some limitations are essential for the protection of the right of freedom of speech and of the press and the interests of the public in having a free dissemination of news and information. None of these rights are without qualification. Courts have encountered considerable difficulty in seeking to balance these conflicting interests. In almost every case involving assertion of a right of privacy, the court is called upon to resolve a conflict between the rights of the individual on the one hand and the interests of society on the other.

Next, the court quoted from 41 *American Jurisprudence:*

> In order to constitute an invasion of the right of privacy, an act must be of such a nature as a reasonable man can see might and probably would cause mental distress and injury to anyone possessed of ordinary feelings and intelligence, situated in like circumstances as the complainant. . . . .

Applying these ideas to the facts of the case, the court concluded that giving birth by a twelve-year-old was unusual; that it was a biological occurrence that would naturally excite public interest; that the event was required by law to be entered into the public records anyway; and that the right of privacy could not be called upon to protect super-sensitiveness. It seems that public excitement is more important than individual repose, and that twelve-year-old mothers who shun publicity are supersensitive. Such applications of an avowed doctrine pay merely lip service to a neglected right.

Books

Aside from the New York cases involving books, only one other reported case can be discussed under this category. The case deals with the question as to whether or not a pen portrait of a relatively unknown person in a novel is an invasion of privacy.

The plaintiff was a resident and native of a small community in Florida. In her complaint, she alleged that she had lived a quiet private life, shunning and avoiding notoriety and publicity; that defendant, a well-known novelist, had published a widely distributed novel which included a biographical sketch, description and partial life history of the plaintiff, as a component part of the book; and that, as a result of the publication, plaintiff's personality had been invaded by exposure, her name had been cheapened, her peace of mind had been disturbed, and she had been caused to suffer from contempt, ridicule, humiliation, great mental pain, and personal injury. She demanded judgment for $100,000 damages. Her complaint specified four grounds for action, and the defendant demurred to all. The demurrer was sustained, but on appeal the order sustaining the demurrer as to the action for invasion of privacy was reversed. As a basis for its decision to reverse, the appellate court referred, among other things, to the fourth section of the Florida Declaration of Rights:

> All courts in this state shall be open, so that every person for any injury done him in his lands, goods, person or reputation shall have remedy, by due course of law, and right and justice shall be administered without sale, denial or delay.

The court then gave its interpretation:

> The word "person" . . . should not be confined to the person's physical body alone. The individual has a mind and spirit as well as a body. He has thoughts, emotions and feelings, as well as physical sensations. So, the word "person" as used in said section, must be construed to mean the whole man, his personality as well as his physical body.

The case then went back to the trial court for trial. This was in 1944. The trial later took place and resulted in judgment for the defendant. Plaintiff appealed, and the appellate court had another ruling to make in 1947. This time the court was concerned with a particular plea, set forth by the defendant, which seemed to lie at the basis of the trial court's judgment against the plaintiff. Addressing itself to this plea, the court gave its opinion:

> In analyzing this Amended Plea 17, it does not appear to meet the test set forth by the authorities. The plea seeks to justify the publication of this matter concerning the plaintiff because of the fame of the author, the widespread distribution of the book, the general acceptance of the book by many people, both in America and abroad, and because of the great literary merit and popularity of the book. The plea does not allege that there was a legitimate public interest in the plaintiff. The eminence of the defendant as an author and the excellence of her writings afford no basis for her privilege to destroy the right of privacy accorded by law to the plaintiff. Nor can the defendant create a public interest in an area or a community, and thereby justify the invasion of privacy of one who happens to live in that particular area or community.

After thus rejecting the defendant's attempt to justify her unauthorized portrayal of the plaintiff, the court made its ruling. The judgment of the trial court was reversed, and a new trial was ordered, with directions that plaintiff be allowed to recover only nominal damages and costs. Why was her recovery confined to nominal damages? Because, according to the court, the evidence did not show that she had suffered substantial damages, her health had not been impaired and, in fact, she had gained twenty pounds. Besides, while she complained of being teased and thought the publication had upset her, the evidence did not show that she had suffered mental anguish, that she had lost any friends or their respect, or that any injury had resulted to her character or reputation. Furthermore, it was not shown that the defendant had acted with malice.

The privacy of an individual concededly had been invaded, and yet the invader was allowed the spoils without assessment. What good was accomplished by saying that everyone was entitled to a remedy for injuries to his person, and that by "person" was meant "the whole man, his personality as well as his physical body"? Surely nominal damages could hardly be considered a remedy. Surely the recognition of privacy in this manner could be classed no higher than a sham.

10

Invasion by Motion Pictures, Radio, and Television

First motion pictures, then radio, and then television have been added as *media* of mass communication. As with other *media,* these too may be used for entertainment or trade purposes, for advertisement, and for the dissemination of educational information. They inevitably make use of personal names, portray personalities, and recount events. What is shown or broadcast may cause the heartstrings of privacy to vibrate, and justification or condemnation will follow. Aside from the revelation of private affairs and the exploitation of personalities, perhaps the deepest disturbance is caused by the revival of a forgotten past.

Motion Pictures

The right of privacy was recognized by the highest court of California, for the first time, in 1931. The case arose as the result of a motion picture called *The Red Kimono.* There was a time when the plaintiff lived the life of a prostitute. During that period of her life, she was tried for murder and acquitted. In 1919, she abandoned her shameful ways and became rehabilitated to normal living. In 1919, she married and began caring for her home as an ordinary housewife, living an exemplary, virtuous, and righteous life. She assumed her place in respectable society and made many friends. Then in 1925, like a bomb out of nowhere, came the motion picture. It was based on the true story of her past life. While her maiden name was used in the picture, the name she had acquired by marriage was used in advertisements, which described the film as the true story of the "unsavory incidents" in her life. She complained that the picture had caused her friends to scorn and abandon her, and that it had exposed her to obloquy, contempt, and ridicule, resulting in grievous mental and physical suffering.

This being a new question for the California court, the views of other jurisdictions were first consdered, and then came the following conclusions:

In the absence of any provision of law, we would be loath to conclude that

125

the right of privacy as the foundation for an action in tort, in the form known and recognized in other jurisdictions, exists in California. We find, however, that the fundamental law of our state contains provisions which, we believe, permit us to recognize the right to pursue and obtain safety and happiness without improper infringements thereon by others.

Section 1 of article 1 of the Constitution of California provides as follows: "All men are by nature free and independent, and have certain inalienable rights, among which are those of enjoying and defending life and liberty; acquiring, possessing and protecting property; and pursuing and obtaining safety and happiness."

The right to pursue and obtain happiness is guaranteed to all by the fundamental law of our state. This right by its very nature includes the right to live free from the unwarranted attack of others upon one's liberty, property, and reputation. Any person living a life of rectitude has that right to happiness which includes a freedom from unnecessary attacks on his character, social standing, or reputation.

The use of appellant's true name in connection with the incidents of her former life in the plot and advertisements was unnecessary and indelicate, and a willfull and wanton disregard of that charity which should actuate us in our social intercourse, and which should keep us from unnecessarily holding another up to the scorn and contempt of upright members of society.

Thus, in California, the right of privacy was initially recognized as a component part of the right to pursue and obtain happiness. The case in which this view was announced was a perfect example of infringement. As shown by another later case, the right so conceived was not to be considered as one without limitations.

In 1945, a staff sergeant in the Marine Corps participated in the invasion of Iwo Jima. Some time later, a Hollywood studio produced *Sands of Iwo Jima,* a motion picture which, according to the sergeant, depicted certain incidents, circumstances, and conditions encountered by him while serving as an enlisted man in the Marine Corps. He alleged that the portrayal was partly factual and partly fictional, that the picture was advertised as re-enacting certain incidents in his life and activities, that he was not consulted, that his consent was neither sought nor given, and that his privacy had thereby been invaded. So here was a man who would not have thought of complaining about any news reports of his activities as a figure in the war effort, but when he found a motion picture corporation making capital of his personality he wanted to share in the profits to the extent of $150,000. He failed in the attempt, because he would not state, by ultimate facts instead of conclusions, what portions of the picture were fictional. According to the court, it was perfectly all right to produce and exhibit a motion picture based upon the public activities of an individual so long as the portrayal was factual.

It is difficult to conceive of any Hollywood production as consisting of an entirely factual portrayal, unless the photography is accomplished at the scene of and at the time of the incident. Furthermore, to base the outcome of a privacy action upon a narrow margin of difference between fact and fiction seems a bit arbitrary. If the portrayal is fictional, there can be no question as to whether or not there has been an invasion, for in such case the conclusion is drawn that a use of personality has been made for trade purposes through furnishing of entertainment. But if the portrayal is factual, consideration should be given to the question as to the purpose which prompted the production. If the aim is to enlighten, the portrayal is justified. However, if the aim is to seek profit by offering entertainment, then the portrayal should be deemed an exploitation of personality, an invasion of privacy.

Fiction does not always lead to a recognition of invasion. This was discovered by the members of a family who received little comfort from a Federal court whose 1944 decision was based upon Massachusetts law. The motion picture was called *Primrose Path*. A stage play bearing the same name was found to be the source of the plot and characters. The stage play was in turn based upon a novel entitled *February Hill*. The author of the book had grown up as a playmate of one member of the family and knew the family well. The book was written about that family. As has often been the case, many details were omitted from the picture, the locale was changed, the name of the hill on which the characters lived was changed, and the cause of the father's death was changed. As described by the court, the book and the play were merely sources of the incidents, plot, and characterization, but the portrayal was such that the characters would not be identified with the family involved. The court also pointed out that the action was being brought on the motion picture and not on the book. Should that have made a difference, if the one was the origin of the other? Certainly an intelligent reader could make the identification. The court noted that the personality of the father had been retained in the picture, but hastened to add:

> This is the probable cause of the great emotional distress of the plaintiffs upon seeing the picture. There is, however, no action in this state for the libel of a dead man or the hurt feelings of his family.

It was also pointed out that the right of privacy was not recognized in

Massachusetts except under the broad definition of libel, which included publications that served to discredit a person in the minds of any considerable and respectable class in his community. The troubled family was not considered to have fallen within that definition.

Shakespeare said through Antony: "The evil that men do lives after them, the good is oft interred with their bones. . . ." A former prostitute, a marine sergeant, and a private family came to the bar of justice to plead their respective causes. Only the first went home victorious. The evil that men do may later bring reward, the good is oft converted to a stranger's purse.

Radio and Television

Here are two powerful *media* of communication which can reach the attention of millions in an instant. Except on rare occasions, the main activities of these media have been almost exclusively confined to the area of entertainment. The commercial provides the pause for refreshment. Detective stories are among the main sources of attraction.

On March 22, 1937, a chauffeur was held up by a robber and shot. Aside from his serious injury and severe shock, he became mentally ill, nervous, and distraught. Mere mention of the shooting caused him acute nervous attacks. On August 4, 1938, the story was dramatized on a radio program known by the title *Calling All Cars*. Unaware of what was to take place, the chauffeur sat listening to his radio, and when his story came over the air, his past suffering revisited him, and his mental anguish was aggravated by telephone calls from sympathetic friends who were desirous of rehashing what he had wanted to forget. His condition became worse, he was unable to drive, and he lost his job. A Federal court in California decided in his favor. It would have been a pity if the law to be applied had been that of a state in which the right of privacy was not recognized.

The Big Story is another program which has dealt with incidents in the lives of individuals. This program has been centered around the praiseworthy efforts of newspapermen, sometimes in bringing criminals to justice, and sometimes in aiding persons to gain their freedom. In 1955, a Federal court in the District of Columbia was faced with the task of deciding a case that arose out of a *Big Story* telecast.

The story began in 1919, when the plaintiff was convicted of bank robbery in Minnesota. He received a forty-year sentence. After serving for nine years, he was paroled and pardoned. In 1933, he was tried and convicted of first degree murder in the District of Columbia. His sentence was death. He lost an appeal in 1934, and the Supreme Court refused to review the case. A number of interested persons and committees and a female reporter, who worked for a Washington newspaper, went to work in his behalf, and in 1935 his sentence was commuted to life imprisonment. In 1940, he received a conditional release from his life sentence, and in 1945 he was given a pardon by the President. In 1936 or 1937, a detective magazine carried an article on the case. In 1948, a fictionalized version of the story was told through a radio program, and the story given was so similar to the facts that plaintiff and others easily identified it with that of the plaintiff. In 1952, with the consent of the newspaperwoman who was being honored by the program, the story was retold in fictionalized form through *The Big Story*. The plaintiff was not consulted. When he heard of the intended telecast, he requested the broadcasting company not to air the story, but his request was ignored. Plaintiff brought action and stated in his complaint, among other things, that he had led an exemplary life since the day of his pardon; that he had been a governmental employee from 1940 to 1945; that he had operated a resort lodge in Virginia from 1945 to 1951; and that he had again become a governmental employee in 1953, rooming in Washington while maintaining his family home in Virginia. The court viewed the telecast in this way:

> The telecast here involved was one of a series of similar dramatizations, commending the accomplishments of newspaper reporters in bringing criminals to justice or in securing the release of innocent persons convicted of crime. In each of the programs the actual name of the reporter and his paper were used, but the names of other persons portrayed were changed, and the incidents were fictionalized for dramatic effect.

Viewing the telecast in the light of the true story, the court observed:

> Thus, the points of similarity between the plaintiff's life and the television story . . . are reduced to: a conviction in the District of Columbia of first-degree murder in connection with the shooting of a gambler in Washington; failure to call a "common-law wife" as an alibi witness; Miss ——'s effective interest in providing the defendant's innocence; securing of other counsel after the trial; emotional turmoil of the convicted man while awaiting execution; additional evidence as to the leaves in front of an eyewitness' apartment window; another eyewitness coming forward, after affirmance of the conviction, to state that defendant was not the murderer; thanking of Miss —— by the defendant after his release; and the physical resemblance between the actor and the plaintiff as he was twenty years ago.

The case having been brought in a Federal Court, it was necessary to determine what law was applicable. On this matter, the court said:

The tort of invasion of privacy being a personal injury, the question whether plaintiff has a cause of action on the facts stated by him should be determined by the law of the jurisdiction where he sustained the injury . . . . The injury in these cases is the humiliation and outrage to plaintiff's feelings, resulting from the telecast. The last event necessary to make the defendant liable was not the final act in publication of the telecast, as plaintiff argues, but the reaction of the telecast on his own sensibilities.

The reaction, according to the court, would normally be felt at a person's domicile, the place where he spent most of his time and where he had his major contacts. When the plaintiff claimed that the District of Columbia was the place where he had most of his contacts, the court retorted that a decision as to place of injury would make no difference in this case, for the plaintiff had no case either under Virginia law or under that of the District of Columbia.

Virginia has a statute similar to that of New York. It provides every resident of Virginia with a right of action whenever he is portrayed, without his consent, for advertising or trade purposes. It goes further than the New York statute in that it provides that heirs of deceased persons so portrayed shall also have a right of action. The New York courts have held that fictionalized versions of events in the lives of individuals fall within the prohibitions of the statute. Why, then, should a Federal court, applying a similar statute, and conceding a portrayal to be fictional, say that the telecast of such a portrayal does not fall within the statute?

What did the court have to say about the law in the District of Columbia?

Whether a right of action for invasion of privacy exists in the District of Columbia has not been authoritatively determined.

However, the court was willing to recognize the right as defined in the *American Law Reports:*

The unwarranted appropriation or exploitation of one's personality, the publicizing of ones' private affairs with which the public has no legitimate concern, or the wrongful intrusion into one's private activities, in such manner as to outrage or cause mental suffering, shame, or humiliation to a person of ordinary sensibilities.

Using this definition as a basis, the court came to its conclusion:

Under this definition, which embodies the minimum requirements of the many cases there noted, the essential elements of an action for invasion of privacy would be: (1) private affairs in which the public had no concern; (2) publication of such affairs; (3) unwarranted publication, that is, absence of any waiver or privilege authorizing it; and (4) publication such as would cause mental suffering, shame, or humiliation to a person of ordinary sensibilities. As to the first element, the "private affairs" should be at least currently unknown to the public; and as to the second element, publication would necessarily include identification of the facts disclosed with the complainant. The third element, a mixed question of fact and law, and the fourth element, a fact question for the jury, need not be reached if either of the first two elements is not present. On the undisputed facts disclosed by the various pleadings and admissions before the court on this motion, it is clear that the first two essential elements of a cause of action are lacking in the case at bar.

It seems strange that the court should express its willingness to adopt a definition and then proceed to distort it. Does not the definition state, as the first and separate method by which an invasion of privacy may be recognized, "The unwarranted appropriation or exploitation of one's personality"? Can any grammatical reading of the definition lead one to conclude that "private affairs in which the public had no concern" is an essential element? At most, only two requirements are laid down, and not four; either an "unwarranted appropriation or exploitation of one's personality," or "the publicizing of one's private affairs with which the public has no legitimate concern," or "the wrongful intrusion into one's private activities;" and "in such manner as to outrage or cause mental suffering, shame, or humiliation to a person of ordinary sensibilities."

There was no doubt that the story portrayed was that in which the plaintiff had played a leading role. There was no doubt that the presentation was one affected by dramatization and fictionalization. There could be no doubt that the production was aimed at serving a commercial purpose. Since the plaintiff had not been consulted, his personality was surely appropriated and exploited. And since no public interest was served, such appropriation and exploitation were unwarranted.

Not all complaints arise out of prominent portrayals of personalities. Sometimes what may appear as a mere slip of the tongue results in a claim of invasion. An example of this is found in *Cohen v. Marx,* a California case decided in 1949. Every radio listener and television viewer is familiar with the program called *You Bet Your Life.* Even more familiar is the talent of Groucho Marx. He is a master in the art of entertaining through interviews. During the course of such interviews, he often recalls personal experiences, which he relates in a manner that provokes laughter. Perhaps now he is a bit more cautious when personalities come to mind, even though the California court decided in his favor.

The court reviewed Cohen's statement of facts as follows:

In 1933, he had entered the prize ring as a professional boxer under the name of "Canvasback Cohen"; that he continued this ring career, losing decisions, until about 1939, when he abandoned the prize ring as a career; that on January 12, 1949, defendant Groucho Marx broadcast over a program of the defendant A. B. C. on its program "You Bet Your Life," "I once managed a prize-fighter, Canvasback Cohen. I brought him out here, he got knocked out, and I made him walk back to Cleveland."

The remark touched the tickling apparatus of the audience, but how did it affect the sensibilities of Mr. Cohen? The court felt that only persons who owned a right to privacy had a right to allow their sensibilities to be affected. The question to which the court addressed itself was whether or not Cohen had waived his right of privacy by entering the prize ring:

This question must be answered in the affirmative. A person who by his accomplishments, fame or mode of life, or by adopting a profesison or calling which gives the public a legitimate interest in his doings, affairs, or character, is said to become a public personage, and thereby relinquishes a part of his right of privacy . . . .

Applying the foregoing rule to the facts in the present case it is evident that when plaintiff sought publicity and the adulation of the public, he relinquished his right of privacy on matters pertaining to his professional activity, and he could not at his will and whim draw himself like a snail into his shell and hold others liable for commenting upon the acts which had taken place when he voluntarily exposed himself to the public eye. As to such acts he had waived his right of privacy and he could not at some subsequent period rescind his waiver.

For what reason does the public gain a legitimate interest in the affairs of an individual? One who seeks public patronage asks the public to invest in his career. The public is, therefore, entitled to know the qualifications of the candidate, as well as the status and result of the investment. To the extent that the public is kept informed concerning these matters the invididual has no cause for complaint. But when the purpose served is the profit of a private commercial enterprise, and when the purpose of the revelation is to amuse rather than to inform, then the portrayal of even a public personage cannot be justified on the ground that he is one in whom the public has a legitimate interest. This view does not seem to have been considered in *Cohen v. Marx.*

Another boxer found the courtroom to be an additional arena in which to taste defeat. Ettore and Louis met in a Philadelphia prize ring on September 22, 1936. The bout lasted for five rounds, and Louis remained the champion. Motion pictures were taken of the fight, and Ettore received $500 from the movie proceeds. On December 30, 1949, and again on December 8, 1950, portions of the movie were telecast on the program called *Greatest Fights of the Century*. Thereafter, Ettore brought action against the television broadcasting company and the sponsors of the program. The Federal District Court of the Eastern District of Pennsylvania gave its decision in 1954.

The court found it unnecessary to decide what law should be applied, for in its opinion the law of no state would allow Ettore a favorable decision. Said the court:

> It is the conclusion of this Court that the right of privacy was lost by virtue of plaintiff's performance and further that by reason of being a public figure, the plaintiff cannot claim an invasion of his right of privacy, since the publication in question only pertained to his professional career. This court further concludes that the immunity from liability is not lost through lapse of time. A subject of public interest can be brought again to public attention later on.
>
> Having determined that the plaintiff has no cause of action for violation of his right of privacy at common law, this Court concludes that there is no right of recovery under the Right of Privacy section of the New York Civil Rights Law.

It is obvious that the court viewed the common law right of privacy as encompassing only the immunity from exposure. Commercial exploitation was not considered. And the court applied its common law view to its interpretation of the New York statute. It should be noted that a Federal District Court in New York took an opposite view four years before in *Sharkey v. National Broadcasting Co., Inc.* That case also arose from a movie shown on *Greatest Fights of the Century*.

The right of privacy should be viewed as both a personal and a property right. When Ettore contended that his property rights had been invaded, the court replied that a professional athlete had no property right in his performance; that practical difficulties would be involved if all athletes had property rights in their performances; and that:

> Radio and television rights are held by the ball club or promoter and not by the individual player or participant.

The fact that Ettore received $500 from the movie proceeds should indicate that a right had been bargained away in return for this price. The fact that a bargain had been entered into should indicate that certain limitations were contemplated by the parties to the contract. There was no television in 1936. At that time, it could hardly be contemplated that movies taken of a fight would be used for any other purpose than their exhibition in movie houses. Would it then be reasonable to conclude that Ettore had bargained away his television rights when he bargained away his movie rights? Some actors and actresses, whose old films have been shown on television, have expressed their feelings on the subject, but to date no official action has been taken.

Once in a while a person loses his head and conducts himself in a manner that disturbs the peace of a community. The incident is given wide publicity, and then the community gradually settles back to normalcy. If later pertinent to a particular study, the incident may be recalled, but in a world overflowing with commercial ambitions, someone seizes the opportunity of treating the incident as fertile material for planting in the field of entertainment. The view taken with respect to such operation may coldly favor the enterprising operator, treating the incident as falling within the scope of the public domain, or it may compassionately protect the personality of the individual affected. Even an offender has rights. A murderer is buried after execution, not cast out as nurture for birds of prey.

A 1956 California case dealt with a *Dragnet* broadcast based upon such an incident. The plaintiff was the operator of a carnival and animal show. Some mental disturbance must have caused him suddenly to notify the Los Angeles police that a black panther, which had been placed on a truck for transportation, had disappeared. A citywide and countywide search began. The community was frightened. As suddenly as the original report was made, it was later withdrawn. The plaintiff was arrested and subjected to a psychiatric examination. Three months later, the story was retold on the radio program called *Dragnet*. The plaintiff contended that this broadcast caused his previous nervousness to be revived and his friends to desert him. Conceding that the incident had news value at the time of its occurrence, the plaintiff contended that such value had been lost by the passage of time. After making clear its view that only the private life of an individual was entitled to protection, the court concluded:

> It is a characteristic of every era, no less than of our contemporary world, that events which have caught the popular imagination or incidents which have aroused the public interest, have been frequently revivified long after their occurrence in the literature, journalism, or other media of communication of a later day. These events, being embedded in the communal history are proper material for such recounting. It is well established, therefore, that the mere passage of time does not preclude the

publication of such incidents from the life of one formerly in the public eye which are already public property.

The case that established the right of privacy in California (previously discussed) involved a motion picture which retold the past life of a former prostitute, who had found herself in the public eye. But the court in that case did not follow the principle that "old news never dies." Perhaps the distinction between the cases lies in the fact that the name of the former prostitute was used in the movie and its advertisement, while the name of the carnival operator was not used in the story told by *Dragnet*. Should this make a difference, especially when the *Dragnet* program was broadcast only three months after the incident upon which it was based? Is not identity the element that is established by the use of a name? And cannot identity be established without the use of a name?

Speaking of news, we must not overlook the fact that radio and television are used as *media* for the dissemination of news. Usually these *media* tell little more than what is found in the daily newspaper. Some commentators seek to reveal the hidden fact and, in so doing, at times provoke complaints of individuals affected.

A Federal court in the District of Columbia was confronted by one such complaint in 1945. The plaintiff was a defendant in a sedition case which was receiving wide publicity. A news commentator, in a radio broadcast, spoke about the case and mentioned the fact that the plaintiff was working as a bartender and waiter at a Washington hotel, thus being in a position to overhear conversations between high officials of the Government. Now, if such revelation was meant as evidence bearing upon the guilt of the accused, it should have been brought out in open court and not over the radio. On the other hand, if it was meant as a warning against possible danger to the public interest, it was quite proper. It seems that the court took the latter view in denying relief to the complaining party.

What is said about a person over the radio can be well thought out in advance, and motion pictures taken of news events can be edited before being shown on television. Unless discretion is diligently exercised, there are bound to be complaints.

The plaintiff in a Florida case, decided in 1955, had found himself the recipient of unwanted publicity. He was on his way home one day when he stopped at the cigar shop in a hotel. As he was looking over the newsstand, he was suddenly pushed against a wall by one of several men who had moved in fast. He was then subjected to questioning. A subsequent news telecast contained the showing of a "canned" film depicting a gambling raid on a Miami Beach restaurant, followed by another raid on a hotel in the same city. A narrative account accompanied the film. The film showed the plaintiff standing against a wall, with one or two men, presumably officers, talking to him. The picture of the plaintiff and the officers occupied the entire screen, with a corner of the cigarette counter visible in some of the shots. The scene, consuming several seconds, was flashed on immediately after the restaurant scene.

After holding that a television company had a qualified privilege to use the name or photograph of any person who had become an "actor" in a newsworthy event, and that a television company should be held to the same degree of care with regard to privacy as was expected of newspaper publishers and producers of motion pictures, wherever the telecaster had the same opportunity to edit and cut, the court evaluated the plaintiff's position:

> Even though the plaintiff's role of "actor" in an event having news value was not of his own volition—having been thrust upon him by the investigating officers by mistake—the fact remains that he was in a public place and present at a scene where news was in the making. He was not "tagged" as a gambler; his name was not mentioned; the most that can be said is that his presence at the scene was under ambiguous and, perhaps, suspicious circumstances. But certainly those of his friends and acquaintances who saw his picture on the screen would know that there was nothing sinister about his presence there. Further, the background of his picture clearly showed him to be at a newsstand and not at some residential apartment, and that he occupied the role that, in fact, was his. If not, a simple explanation by him would make this clear. We see nothing humiliating or embarrassing in such a role—shopping at a newsstand—nor anything that would offend a person of "ordinary sensibilities."

As to the matter of care, the court observed that it took courts months to find facts, while reporters were expected to find and determine facts in a matter of hours or even minutes. It was only reasonable, therefore, to expect occasional errors. And the preservation of American democracy depended on the speedy receipt of information by the public.

Much is excused and justified in the name of democracy. What is so important about the publication of facts whose truth is in doubt? Surely it is enough to report that a raid has taken place, without exposing an innocent bystander to possible misconceptions of his role. Get a story! Get a picture! These are the cries. All right! Get the story, and take the picture, but think before you publish. Is the object to fill space, or to sensationalize, or to attract, or to amuse? Or is the object to inform, or to advocate, or to protect? What purpose will be served by the portrayal? Is it important? Is it so important that the rights of an individual must be sacrificed? If the individual must bow to the publisher's conception of public demands, where is democracy? If the individual is the last to be considered, where is democracy? If speed is more important than accuracy, instinct more important than reason, and curiosity more important than privacy, where is democracy?

11

Invasion by Publicity Concerning One Deceased

If the right of privacy is regarded as a personal right, it must necessarily die with the person. If, on the other hand, it is viewed as a property right, it may descend to those eligible to share in the estate of the deceased. Looking at the matter from still another point of view, a close relative of one deceased may be considered as having a relational right of privacy. Regardless of viewpoint, survivors of dearly departed have had little success in cases based upon alleged invasions by publicity concerning the dead. In fact, aside from a Georgia case discussed in Chapter VI, evidence of such success can be found in only one other reported case, and that case, *Douglas v. Stokes* (1912), was decided by a Kentucky court.

The case centered around the conduct of a photographer who had been called upon to photograph the bodies of deceased twins. Twin boys had been born to the plaintiffs. They were attached together from their shoulders down to the ends of their bodies. Although they had one set of bowels and one breast bone, they were otherwise twins and not one baby. They soon died, and their father employed the defendant to photograph them and to make twelve copies of the picture. The defendant obliged, but while he was at it he made extra copies and filed one in the copyright office. Not only did the court deny his claim of copyright, but it agreed with the plaintiffs that the conduct of the defendant constituted an invasion of their right of privacy. Said the court:

> We do not see that this case can be distinguished from those involving the like use of the photograph of a living person, and this has been held actionable.

The core of the case lies in the depth of the following expression uttered by the court:

> The most tender affections of the human heart cluster about the body of one's dead child. A man may recover for any injury or indignity done the body, and it would be a reproach to the law if physical injuries might be recovered for, and not those incorporeal injuries which would cause much greater suffering and humiliation.

Another case involving the photograph of a deceased person was decided by a California court in 1939. On the surface, what transpired would seem to be routine and justified, but an examination of the details called for more deliberate consideration. The plaintiff's wife had committed suicide by jumping from a twelfth floor fire escape of an office building in downtown Los Angeles. Her picture appeared in the *Los Angeles Examiner* along with the story. Being used to seeing such publicity in the papers, who would even think of bringing action on account of it? But there was more to the case.

Things happened between the time of the suicide and the publication of the picture. Plaintiff learned of the suicide when he returned home from work that day. He immediately went to the coroner's office. There he encountered reporters who engaged him in conversation. Upon returning home, he found that the screen to the kitchen window had been forced open, and that the picture of his wife had been taken. He called the editor of the *Examiner* and, getting no satisfaction over the phone, he made another trip downtown and made a further plea against the proposed publication. His pleas were in vain. He was told that the picture was in the possession of the homicide squad of the police department. Thereafter, the stolen picture was published.

Plaintiff brought his action against the *Examiner*. He had no proof that agents of the *Examiner* had broken into his house and taken the picture, and so his case was based on what he called his relational right of privacy—a right to be spared unhappiness through publicity concerning another person because of one's relationship to such person.

The court was unwilling to accept the notion of a relational right, asserting that the right of privacy was a personal right, and that one who complained of invasion would have to show that his own privacy had been invaded. And even if the court were willing to recognize a relational right, it felt that its decision could not be favorable to the plaintiff. For one thing, no privacy could be claimed where an event could not remain private. For another thing, the manner of death imposed a duty on the coroner to make an official investigation and became a proper subject of official inquiry. Lastly, the act of committing suicide caused all right of privacy to be waived, whether such right be relational or otherwise.

He had lost his wife, and the last symbol of the privacy they had shared was embodied in the photograph which was his to cherish in his solitude. He could not prevent the story from being published, but he could avoid the further pain of pictorial publicity. Except through the puncture of his privacy the publication of the portrait could not have been accomplished. And if the right was his by relation, how could it have been waived except by his own expression or conduct?

In 1948, an Alabama court indicated its recognition of a relational right of privacy, but could not bring itself to decide in favor of the plaintiffs because of the particular facts of the case. The case arose out of a commercial radio program called *Tuscaloosa Town Talks.* One such program was devoted to the telling of a story which held the interest of the listening audience, but which disturbed certain persons connected with the central character.

The story went back to 1905, when a Tuscaloosa blacksmith lived happily and prosperously with his wife and two daughters. One day, he announced to his family that he was going to Birmingham to purchase materials for his shop. He hitched a pair of mules to an old-fashioned surrey and, having withdrawn all of the $700.00 which had been deposited in the local bank, was on his way. Late that night, a shot was fired in the vicinity of a nearby bridge. Investigation revealed that the shot had penetrated the surrey of the blacksmith. His coat was found with a bullet hole in it. A billfold was also found, and it was his, and it was empty. A fellow townsman found the mules and brought them back to town. Suspicion of murder fell upon this man. He was arrested and spent five months in jail, while attempts were being made to gather evidence against him. The attempts failed, and he was finally released, but the public still believed that he had murdered the blacksmith. The river had been dragged, and every inch for miles around had been searched, but to no avail. Twenty-five years later, the body of the blacksmith came back to Tuscaloosa. He had died of cancer in California after accumulating considerable wealth. One of his daughters had been named the principal beneficiary in his will.

This was the story told on a commercial program. The dramatic facts must have held the audience spellbound, but the daughters of the blacksmith felt a piercing in their heart. It would be difficult to deny that the public had an interest in the story, just as it would be difficult to deny that the daughters had an interest in its suppression. The public was entitled to the story as a matter of information, but if its telling was prompted by the gain of exploitation the innocent victims should not have been left to feast on sympathy alone. The court did not make this distinction in the rendering of its decision:

> In the case at bar however much we may sympathize with the feelings of the plaintiffs, we consider that the broadcast was the subject of legitimate public interest. By his own acts ———— ———— made himself a public char-

acter. The passage of time could not give privacy to his acts because the
story of ——— ——— is a part of the history of the community. It is em-
bedded in the public record through the imprisonment of ——— ———
on a charge of murder and his fight in the courthouse to prove his in-
nocence and to free himself from the stigma of that charge. The will of
——— ——— is a public record. The broadcast was based on fact. We see
no reason why the right of privacy of daughters might not be violated
by unwarranted and offensive publicity with reference to their deceased
father, but conclude for the reasons given that the allegations in this
case do not state a cause of action.

Thus, according to the Alabama court, unwarranted and offensive
publicity concerning one deceased would give his children a cause of
action for violation of their right of privacy. It would seem that parents
of a deceased child would have a similar right under such circumstances.
Would the pubilcation of a picture taken of the dead body of a fifteen-
year-old girl, killed in an automobile accident, be considered unwarranted and offensive? Here is the answer given by the Massachusetts
court in 1951:

Assuming for the purposes of this case that the plaintiffs have a right of
privacy, we fail to see how it was impaired by what the defendant did.
Doubtless many persons at such a time would be distressed or annoyed by
a publication of the sort here involved. It is a time above all others when
they would prefer to be spared the anguish of wide or sensational publicity. But if the right asserted here were sustained, it would be difficult
to fix its boundaries. A newspaper account or a radio broadcast setting
forth in detail the harrowing circumstances of the accident might well be
as distressing to the members of the victim's family as a photograph of
the sort described in the declaration. A newspaper could not safely publish the picture of a train wreck or of an airplane crash if any of the
bodies of the victims were recognizable. The law does not provide a remedy for every annoyance that occurs in everyday life. Many things which
are distressing or may be lacking in propriety or good taste are not actionable. Moreover, if the parents had a cause of action in a case like the
present there would seem to be no reason why other members of the immediate family, the brothers and sisters, whose sensibilities may also have
been wounded should not also be permitted to sue. The only reference
to the plaintiffs was that the girl whose body appeared in the photograph
was their daughter. This can hardly be said to interfere with their privacy.
At least, if there is such a right in this Commonwealth we would not be
prepared to extend it to a case like the present.

Such has been the attitude taken by the courts in balancing the
rights of the press against the rights of individuals. First, they recognize the predicament of those in mourning, the yearning for silence
and solemnity, the aggravation of sensational publicity. Then they

throw up their hands and reiterate the cry that it is difficult to set boundaries, and that an opening of the gates would be accompanied by a greater volume of complaints. Is justice assured by the avoidance of difficulty? Would not a rush of complaints be curtailed by imposition of restraints upon sensationalism?

The same treatment was accorded by an Iowa court, in 1956, to the aggrieved parents of a deceased eight-year-old boy. The boy had been missing for a month. The story of his finding was top rank news. There would have been no complaint if a certain photograph had not accompanied the story. A local newspaper contained the photograph showing the mutilated and decomposed body of the boy. Had its inevitable effect upon the parents been considered before publication? Was its publication so vital to the public interest?

The majority of the court found in favor of the publisher on the ground that the publication of the photograph was justified, it being in connection with a matter of legitimate public interest. A strong minority of three dissenters spoke through one of its members:

> I also cannot agree with the application of this rule by the courts of Georgia and Alabama in their apparent determination that pictures of news interest, no matter how morbid and repulsive they may be, or how much they may needlessly hurt anyone concerned, are privileged and that publishers are thereafter governed solely by their own consciences and sense of decency in determining whether or not such pictures are printed.

It is not only by morbid and repulsive pictures of the dead that surviving relatives may sense an invasion of privacy, but any portrayal that smacks of exploitation may move such survivors to action. An example is given in *Donahue v. Warner Bros. Pictures Distributing Corp.,* a Utah case decided in 1954.

Action was brought by the widow and daughters of Jack Donahue following the portrayal of his life in the movie entitled *Look for the Silver Lining.* The musical show was based primarily on the life of Marilyn Miller, and secondarily on the life of Donahue. The two had co-starred in two famous Broadway productions, *Sunny* and *Rosalie.*

Utah has a privacy statute similar to that of New York and Virginia. The New York statute applies only to living persons. The Utah and Virginia statutes, while containing the same prohibitions as does the New York statute, also prohibit the portrayal of deceased persons, for advertising or trade purposes, without the written consent of their heirs or personal representatives.

The New York courts, as we have seen, have interpreted the New

York statute as drawing a line of demarcation between uses for educational or informative purposes, and uses for advertising or trade purposes. Aside from direct uses of names and pictures in advertisements and in connection with the ordinary products offered for sale, fictional portrayals and factual portrayals meant for amusement have been considered as uses for trade purposes. It seems, therefore, that if the New York view were to be applied to the *Donahue* case, the plaintiffs would win. However, the line of reasoning adopted by the Utah court led to the opposite conclusion.

Since the Utah statute was passed in 1909, and since it was patterned after the New York statute, the court felt that the Utah statute should be interpreted as the New York statute had been interpreted up to the time of the enactment in Utah. It so happened that the only privacy case which had reached the highest New York court after the New York enactment in 1903 and before the Utah enactment in 1909 was the *Rhodes* case (discussed in Chapter V), and it so happened that the *Rhodes* case involved the use of pictures as articles of trade. There had, therefore, been no opportunity for a New York court to offer a broader interpretation than was necessary for the determination of that case. What was that interpretation? The Utah court quoted it as follows:

> Such is the character of the right of privacy preserved by legislation protecting persons against unauthorized use of their names or portraits in the form of advertisements or trade notices. It is a recognition by the lawmaking power of the very general sentiment which prevailed throughout the community against permitting advertisers to promote the sale of their wares by this method, regardless of the wishes of the persons thereby affected.

Was not this statement by the New York court tailored to fit the case at hand? Broadly viewed, did it preclude the consideration of portrayals in movies as coming within the ban of the statute? Even if viewed literally, did it preclude broader interpretations to be made in later cases involving different subject matter?

The Utah court rejected any notion of a distinction between educational and informative portrayals, on the one hand, and fictional portrayals on the other. Such a distinction was too elusive to draw. The legislature could not have meant that such distinction should be drawn. The mandate of the legislature was simple. It was meant to apply only to uses in connection with advertisement and the promotion of sales. The difficulty of distinction left only one of two alternatives to be applied:

This leaves us two alternatives: First to give it a strict and literal application, to prohibit the use of a name, portrait or picture in any manner whatsoever, whether factual or fictional, in connection with any publication where a profit motive is present; or second, the interpretation contended for by defendants, that the statute was intended only to prohibit the use of names, portraits or pictures in connection with advertising or the promotion of the sale of collateral items.

Acceptance of the first alternative, which would include the use of names, pictures, etc., in newspapers, radio, television, newsreels, novels, biographies, plays, movies, etc., would entail the necessity of judicially carving numerous exceptions to skirt the hazards of unconstitutionality because of conflict with the guarantees of freedom of speech and the press. As has been seen, not only is it extremely difficult, if not impossible, to draw out such exceptions with sufficient certainty so that one could safely predict whether a given publication regarding a personality would fall within the statute, but the language of the statute itself provides no basis for any such exceptions. All of which argues that our legislature did not intend any such application of the statute. On the other hand, social considerations, the legislative history of our statute, and its context considered in the light of rules of statutory construction, all point persuasively to the conclusion that the interpretation contended for by the defendant is that which comports with the legislative intent.

The solution of difficult problems does not lie in their dismissal. Success often lies beyond seemingly insurmountable obstacles. Justice cannot always be achieved through the application of simple rules. Complexities must not be allowed to becloud the issue.

12

Invasion by Wiretapping and the Like

We have to choose, and for my part I think it a less evil that some criminals should escape than that the Government should play an ignoble part.

These words were spoken by Justice Holmes as part of his dissenting opinion in the case of *Olmstead v. United States,* decided by the Supreme Court in 1928. His sentiments were shared by three other dissenters: Justices Brandeis, Butler, and Stone.

Olmstead and others had been convicted by a Federal District Court in the State of Washington of conspiracy to violate the National Prohibition Act. The evidence that led to the discovery of the conspiracy had been obtained by four federal prohibition officers through wiretapping. The petitioners contended that the convictions could not stand inasmuch as they had been based upon evidence illegally obtained, hence inadmissible. They claimed that the illegality of the evidence lay in the fact that the practices of the prohibition officers were in violation of the Fourth and Fifth Amendments of the Constitution, as well as in violation of a Washington statute which declared, in effect, that wiretapping was a misdemeanor.

The Fourth Amendment reads:

The right of the people to be secure in their persons, houses, papers, and effects, against unreasonable searches and seizures shall not be violated, and no warrants shall issue, but upon probable cause, supported by oath or affirmation, and particularly describing the place to be searched, and the persons or things to be seized.

The pertinent portion of the Fifth Amendment reads:

. . . nor shall be compelled in any criminal case to be a witness against himself, nor be deprived of life, liberty, or property, without due process of law; . . .

Chief Justice Taft, speaking for the majority, declared that the Fourth and Fifth Amendments had not been violated. There was no question as to the Fifth and, as to the Fourth, the words "persons," "houses," "papers," and "effects" indicated that the searches contemplated encompassed only material things, not such things as telephone

147

conversations. As for the Washington statute, he declared that there was an established common law principle to the effect that the admissibility of evidence was not affected by the illegality of means by which it was obtained. Under these circumstances, the conviction had to be upheld. He added, however, that Congress could legislate against the interception of telephone conversations.

It was then Holmes' turn to speak:

> While I do not deny it, I am not prepared to say that the penumbra of the Fourth and Fifth Amendments covers the defendant, although I fully agree that Courts are apt to err by sticking too closely to the words of a law where those words import a policy that goes beyond them.

The Court, according to Holmes, was not bound in this case by a body of precedents, for no similar situation had theretofore been brought before it. It was, therefore, free to choose its direction. In fact, a choice had to be made between the desire to catch criminals and the desire that the Government not foster and pay for other crimes. "We have to choose," he said, "and for my part I think it a less evil that some criminals should escape than that the Government should play an ignoble part."

Then came Brandeis. Thirty-eight years had passed since his masterful co-authorship of *Right to Privacy*. And privacy still held a most prominent place in his heart. He went further than Holmes, expressing his conviction that the Fourth and Fifth Amendments unquestionably applied to this case. His words rang like a bell to awaken a drowsy community:

> Time works changes, brings into existence new conditions and purposes. Therefore, a principle to be vital must be capable of wider application than the mischief which gave it birth. This is peculiarly true of constitutions. They are not ephemeral enactments, designed to meet passing occasions. They are, to use the words of Chief Justice Marshall "designed to approach immortality as nearly as human institutions can approach it."
>
> .   .   .   .
>
> When the Fourth and Fifth Amendments were adopted, "the form that evil had theretofore taken," had been necessarily simple. Force and violence were then the only means known to man by which a Government could directly effect self-incrimination. It could compel the individual to testify—a compulsion effected, if need be, by torture. It could secure possession of his papers and other articles incident to his private life—a seizure effected, if need be, by breaking and entry. Protection against such invasion of "the sanctities of a man's home and the privacies of life" was provided in the Fourth and Fifth Amendments by specific language.
> . . . . Subtler and more far-reaching means of invading privacy have become available to the Government. Discovery and invention have made

it possible for the Government, by means far more effective than stretching upon the rack, to obtain disclosure in court of what is whispered in the closet.

. . . .

The protection guaranteed by the Amendments is much broader in scope. The makers of our Constitution undertook to secure conditions favorable to the pursuit of happiness. They recognized the significance of man's spiritual nature, of his feelings and of his intellect. They knew that only a part of the pain, pleasure and satisfactions of life are to be found in material things. They sought to protect Americans in their beliefs, their thoughts, their emotions and their sensations. They conferred, as against the Government, the right to be let alone—the most comprehensive of rights and the right most valued by civilized men. To protect that right, every unjustifiable intrusion by the Government upon the privacy of the individual, whatever the means employed, must be deemed a violation of the Fourth Amendment. And the use, as evidence in a criminal proceeding, of facts ascertained by such intrusion must be deemed a violation of the Fifth.

Applying to the Fourth and Fifth Amendments, the established rule of construction, the defendants' objections to the evidence obtained by wiretapping must, in my opinion, be sustained. It is, of course, immaterial where the physical connection with the telephone wires leading into the defendants' premises was made. And it is also immaterial that the intrusion was in aid of law enforcement. Experience should teach us to be most on our guard to protect liberty when the Government's purposes are beneficent. Men born of freedom are naturally alert to repel invasion of their liberty by evil-minded rulers. The greatest dangers to liberty lurk in insidious encroachment by men of zeal, well-meaning but without understanding.

. . . .

To declare that in the administration of the criminal law the end justifies the means—to declare that the Government may commit crimes in order to secure the conviction of a private criminal—would bring terrible retribution. Against that pernicious doctrine this Court should resolutely set its face.

Thus spoke Justice Brandeis. His words, as well as those of Justice Holmes, have not been forgotten. They will always remain as reminders, to those who profess to fight in freedom's cause, that the precious rights sought to be preserved must not be lost in the passionate pursuit of conspirators; and that no justice is achieved when one crime is solved by another.

It took a little time, but in 1934 Congress outlawed wire-tapping by adding section 605 to the Federal Communications Act. The portion which forms the core of the section reads as follows:

. . . no person not being authorized by the sender shall intercept any communication and divulge or publish the existence, contents, substance, purport, effect, or meaning of such intercepted communication to any person. . . .

This law was given its first test in *Nardone v. United States,* decided by the Supreme Court in 1937. Nardone was charged with smuggling, possessing, concealing, and conspiring to smuggle and conceal aoohol in violation of federal law. Evidence to bring about his conviction had been obtained by federal agents through wiretapping. The Government argued that Congress did not mean to tie the arms of law enforcement agencies by the enactment of section 506. The Court, however, speaking through Justice Roberts, felt otherwise:

> It is urged that a construction be given the section which would exclude federal agents, since it is improbable Congress intended to hamper and impede the activities of the government in the detection and punishment of crime. The answer is that the question is one of policy. Congress may have thought it less important that some offenders should go unwhipped of justice than that officers should resort to methods deemed inconsistent with ethical standards and destructive of personal liberty. The same considerations may well have moved the Congress to adopt section 605 as evoked the guaranty against practices and procedures violative of privacy, embodied in the Fourth and Fifth Amendments of the Constitution."

And so it was established, by the *Nardone* case, that evidence obtained by federal agents through wiretapping was inadmissible in the federal courts. Two years later, another *Nardone* case had the same result.

The tragedy that accompanies attempts to establish legal boundaries surrounding lawful conduct is that too often means are devised for circumventing the law. An example of this is found in *Goldman v. United States,* decided by the Supreme Court in 1942.

Section 605 had outlawed wiretapping, and this was held to apply to federal agents in the *Nardone* cases. Now, Goldman had an office in which he conferred with his associates. If you could not tap his phone, what would prevent you from installing a detectaphone in the next office? This device would pick up the conversation and relay it to you. A form of eavesdropping, you might say, and furthermore, Congress had not banned this intriguing method of gathering evidence. Federal agents followed through on this line of thinking, and Goldman was confronted with the evidence thereby obtained. He and his associates argued that section 605 had been violated; that, if it was found that section 605 was not violated, then the *Olmstead* ruling should not be applied, for the cases were distinguishable, and the Olmstead case should be overruled anyway.

The Court held that section 605 did not apply inasmuch as that law prohibited interceptions of telephone communications, not personal conversations.

The petitioners seized upon an observation made in the *Olmstead* case to substantiate their claim that that case was distinguishable from the present one. It was said, in *Olmstead,* that the user of a telephone projects his voice beyond the confines of his home or office and thus assumes a risk of interception. But, argued the petitioners in *Goldman,* such risk is not taken when one speaks to others in an office, intending the conversation to be confined within the four walls.

To this Justice Roberts, speaking for the majority of the Court, replied:

> We think, however, the distinction is too nice for practical application of the Constitutional guarantee, and no reasonable or logical distinction can be drawn between what federal agents did in the present case and state officers did in the Olmstead case.

As for the request that the *Olmstead* decision be overruled, Justice Roberts answered:

> This we are unwilling to do. That case was the subject of prolonged consideration by this court. The views of the court, and the dissenting justices, were expressed clearly and at length. To rehearse and reappraise the arguments pro and con, and the conflicting views exhibited in the opinions, would serve no good purpose. Nothing now can be profitably added to what was there said. It suffices to say that we adhere to the opinion there expressed.

The above does not sound like the same man who delivered the opinion of the Court in the first Nordone case (discussed above).

Chief Justice Stone and Associate Justice Frankfurter joined in a dissenting opinion:

> Had a majority of the Court been willing at this time to overrule the Olmstead case, we should have been happy to join them. But as they have declined to do so, and as we think this case is indistinguishable in principle from Olmstead's, we have no occasion to repeat here the dissenting views in that case with which we agree.

It should be noted that Associate Justice Douglas, who voted with the majority, later regretted his action, as we shall see.

Ten years passed, and then came *On Lee v. United States.* On Lee had been convicted of selling and conspiring to sell a pound of opium.

His conviction had been brought about through the admission of evidence surreptitiously obtained.

On Lee conducted a laundry business. One day Chin Poy, an old acquaintance and former employee, came into the store, and a conversation ensued during which On Lee let slip some incriminating statements. In the words of the Court:

> He did not know that Chin Poy was what the Government calls "an undercover agent" and what petitioner calls a "stool pigeon" for the Bureau of Narcotics. Neither did he know that Chin Poy was wired for sound, with a small microphone in his inside overcoat pocket and a small antenna running along his arm.

Meanwhile, Lawrence Lee, another agent, was stationed outside the store with a receiving set tuned to pick up whatever sounds were transmitted by the microphone in Poy's pocket. Another conversation took place on the street a few days later, with the same apparatus operating. For some reason, Poy was not called as a witness, but Lawrence Lee was (over the objection of On Lee). Was the testimony of Lawrence Lee admissible? It was admitted, and the Supreme Court upheld its admission. The petitioner had no wires which could be tapped, no wireless to be interfered with, and the Court found no law to have been violated by the agents. The conviction was upheld.

The case as reported did not show his alignment, but Justice Black expressed the view that the evidence should have been rejected. Dissenting opinions were written by Justices Frankfurter, Douglas, and Burton. The spirit of Holmes and Brandeis pervades these opinions, small samples of which will suffice to indicate their tenor.

Said Justice Frankfurter:

> The law of this Court ought not to be open to the just charge of having been dictated by the "odious doctrine," as Mr. Justice Brandeis called it, that the end justifies reprehensible means. To approve legally what we disapprove morally, on the ground of practical convenience, is to yield to a shortsighted view of practicality. It derives from a preoccupation with what is episodic and a disregard of long run consequences. The method by which the state chiefly exerts an influence upon the conduct of its citizens, it was wisely said by Archbishop William Temple, is "the moral qualities which it exhibits in its own conduct."

Said Justice Douglas:

> I now more fully appreciate the vice of the practices spawned by *Olmstead* and *Goldman*. Reflection on them has brought new insight to me. I now feel that I was wrong in the *Goldman* case. Mr. Justice Brandeis in his dissent in *Olmstead* espoused the cause of privacy—the right to be let

alone. What he wrote is an historic statement of that proud view. I cannot improve on it.

After quoting at length from Brandeis' dissenting opinion in the *Olmstead* case, Justice Douglas continued:

> That philosophy is applicable not only to a detectaphone placed against the wall or a mechanical device designed to record the sounds from telephone wires but also to the "walky-talky" radio used in the present case. The nature of the instrument that science or engineering develops is not important. The controlling, the decisive factor is the invasion of privacy against the command of the Fourth and Fifth Amendments.

While federal agents were busy gathering evidence by means not held to be illegal, some states sanctioned wiretapping as a method of trapping and convicting suspects. The New York Constitution, as amended in 1938, contains language to that effect. Paragraph 2 of Article 1; section 12, reads as follows:

> The right of the people to be secure against unreasonable interception of telephone and telegraph communications shall not be violated, and ex parte orders or warrants shall issue only upon oath or affirmation that there is reasonable ground to believe that evidence of crime may be thus obtained, and identifying the particular means of communication, and particularly describing the person or persons whose communications are to be intercepted and the purpose thereof.

Working within the framework of this provision, the New York legislature enacted section 813-a of the Code of Criminal Procedure. This section, originally passed in 1942 and amended in 1957, provides that ex parte orders for intercepting communications may be obtained by any district sergeant of any police department of the state, or of any political subdivision thereof, from any justice of a state court or judge of the county court of general sessions of the City of New York.

Texas was very careful in its allowance of wiretapping. Its legislation provided for the exclusion of any evidence obtained in violation, not of federal laws, but of the United States Constitution. Had it excluded evidence obtained in violation of federal laws, section 605 of the Federal Communications Act would have rendered wiretapping evidence inadmissible. On the other hand, the Supreme Court had not considered wiretapping to be in violation of the Constitution.

In the same year that *On Lee v. United States* was decided, 1952, *Schwartz v. Texas* came up for decision before the Supreme Court. A Texas court had convicted Schwartz as an accomplice to a robbery on wiretapping evidence obtained by state agents. Schwartz was a pawnbroker. He entered into a conspiracy with one Jarrett and one Bennett. They were to rob places designated by Schwartz, bring the loot to him, he would dispose of it, and the proceeds would be divided. So they went out and robbed a woman of her jewels and brought them to the pawnbroker. He delayed the settlement, and the conspiracy fell apart. Then, Schwartz tipped off the police as to the whereabouts of Jarrett, and the latter was arrested. After spending two weeks in jail, he consented to phone Schwartz from the sheriff's office. This was part of a scheme to trap Schwartz. With Jarrett's consent, a professional operator set up an induction coil and connected it to a recorder amplifier, which enabled him to overhear and record the conversation. Needless to say, the scheme worked, for it produced the evidence that led to Schwartz's conviction.

The Supreme Court had already decided that wiretap evidence obtained by federal agents was not admissible in the federal courts. Now it was confronted with the question as to whether or not wiretapping evidence obtained by state agents was admissible in state courts. Did section 605 apply to state agents and state court? Remember that the Texas legislature was careful in wording its enactment so as not to outlaw evidence obtained in violation of federal laws, confining its ban to evidence obtained in violation of the Constitution. Remember also that the Supreme Court had already ruled, in previous cases, that wiretapping was not a violation of the Constitution. And so the Court felt that the only question it had to answer was whether or not section 605 should be considered as superseding state laws which sanctioned wiretapping.

Associate Justice Minton spoke for the Court:

> Where a state has carefully legislated so as not to render inadmissible evidence obtained and sought to be divulged in violation of the laws of the United States, this Court will not extend by implication the statute of the United States so as to invalidate the specific language of the state statute. If Congress is authorized to act in a field, it should manifest its intention clearly. It will not be presumed that a federal statute was intended to supersede the exercise of the power of the state unless there is a clear manifestation of intention to do so. The exercise of federal supremacy is not lightly to be presumed.

Thus, it was held, in *Schwartz v. Texas,* that section 605 did not operate to make inadmissible in a state court wiretap evidence obtained by state agents. If the Court had found that Congress intended section 605 to be applicable to evidence offered in state courts, there would have been a further question as to whether or not such legislation lay within the power of Congress to enact. Justice Minton made reference to this question:

> Since we do not believe that Congress intended to impose a rule of evidence on the state courts, we do not decide whether it has the power to do so.

Associate Justice Douglas, who had already taken up the cause of privacy with a vigorous dissent in the *On Lee* case, once again expressed his disagreement with the views of the Court:

> Since, in my view . . ., this wire tapping was a search that violated the Fourth Amendment, the evidence obtained by it should have been excluded. The question whether the Fifth Amendment is applicable to the states . . . probably need not be reached, because a Texas statute has excluded evidence obtained in violation of the Federal Constitution. Therefore, I would reverse the judgment. It is true that the prior decisions of the Court point to affirmance. But those decisions reflect constructions of the Constitution which I think are erroneous. They impinge severely on the liberty of the individual and give the police the right to intrude into the privacy of any life. The practices they sanction have today acquired a momentum that is so ominous I cannot remain silent and bow to the precedents that sanction them.

Five years passed, and during that time Chief Justice Earl Warren had been appointed to head the Court. Under his leadership the Court has taken on a new stature. A new trend in civil rights has been indicated. Abuses of congressional investigations have been checked, segregation has been directed to eventual disappearance, and the torch of privacy has been rekindled.

The first inroads into the activities of state wiretappers were achieved in *Benanti v. United States,* decided by the Supreme Court on December 9, 1957. The decision was unanimous. The case arose through a curious turn of events.

New York police had suspected Benanti of dealing in narcotics. Pursuant to New York law (referred to above), they obtained authority to tap the wires of a bar which Benanti had been known to frequent. One day they intercepted a communication, between Benanti and another, to the effect that "eleven pieces" were to be transported that night. Following up the tip, the police stopped a car being driven by Benanti's brother, but instead of narcotics they found eleven five-gallon cans of alcohol. The cans did not bear tax stamps as required by federal law. So, instead of becoming involved in a state case, Benanti became involved in a federal case. He was later convicted on the evidence that

had been obtained through the wiretapping practiced by state law enforcement officers in accordance with state law.

Chief Justice Warren, who delivered the unanimous opinion of the
Court, saw no alternative but to apply the plain meaning of the words
Congress had chosen to use in section 605. Those words bear repeating:

> . . . . no person not being authorized by the sender shall intercept any
> communication and divulge or publish the existence, contents, substance,
> purport, effect, or meaning of such intercepted communication to any
> person. . . .

In the opinion of the Court, "no person" included not only federal
officers but state officers as well, but what of *Schwartz v. Texas,* wherein
it was held that wiretap evidence obtained by state officers was admissible in a state court? The Government used that case as part of its
argument, and it seemed appropriate that an answer be given. Without
indicating his approval or disapproval of that decision, since it was not
squarely in point, the Chief Justice disposed of the argument in this
fashion:

> The rationale of that case is that despite the plain prohibition of Section
> 605, due regard to Federal-State relations precluded the conclusion that
> Congress intended to thwart a state rule of evidence in the absence
> of a clear indication to that effect. In the instant case we are not dealing
> with a state rule of evidence. Although state agents committed the wire-
> tap, we are presented with a Federal conviction brought about in part by
> a violation of Federal law, in this case in Federal Court.

The full effect of this decision remains to be seen. It now seems
clear that wiretapping, by whomsoever practiced, constitutes a violation
of federal law. Will this stop state officials? Can crime be stopped by
crime? How vigorously will section 605 be enforced against state agents
and those who authorize them? Will *Schwartz v. Texas* be followed
in the future? Perhaps state agents will follow the lead of federal agents
in adopting methods not yet condemned by the Supreme Court, for
even the present Court has condoned what Holmes and Brandeis would
have condemned.

On the same day that *Benanti v. United States* was decided, a divided
Court gave its decision in *Rathbun v. United States.* Rathbun had
been prosecuted and convicted for transmitting an interstate communication in which, it was found, he had threatened the life of a certain
person in order to recover a stock certificate held by the other as collateral for a loan. The communication was made over the telephone,
Rathbun in New York calling Sparks in Colorado. One call having

been made on March 16, 1955, Sparks anticipated another and called the police to listen in through an extension in another room. The call came on the 17th, and the police listened. Evidence thus obtained was admitted at the trial, and the conviction followed. Rathbun sought to have the conviction reversed on the ground that it had been brought about through evidence obtained in violation of section 605.

That wiretapping fell within the meaning of "intercept" there was no doubt, but was listening on an extension an interception? The Court was not faced with the problem of deciding whether or not the use of an extension without the authority of either party to the conversation came within the ban of the statute. Perhaps it would have decided that such use was an unlawful interception. But was it an interception to listen in at the request of the receiver, and without the consent of the sender?

After quoting the portion of section 605 that begins "no person not being authorized by the sender shall intercept . . .," the Court proceeded with its analysis:

> The telephone extension is a widely used instrument of home and office, yet with nothing to evidence congressional intent, petitioner argues that Congress meant to place a severe restriction on its ordinary use by subscribers, denying them the right to allow a family member, an employee, a trusted friend, or even the police to listen to a conversation to which a subscriber is a party. Section 605 points to the opposite conclusion. Immediately following the portion quoted above, the statute continues: " . . . no person not being entitled thereto shall receive or assist in receiving any interstate or foreign communication by wire or radio and use the same or any information therein contained for his own benefit or for the benefit of another not entitled thereto. . . ."
>
> The clear inference is that one entitled to receive the communication may use it for his own benefit or have another use it for him. The communication itself is not privileged, any one party may not force the other to secrecy merely by using a telephone. It has been conceded by those who believe the conduct here violates Section 605 that either party may record the conversation and publish it. The conduct of the party would differ in no way if instead of repeating the message he held out his handset so that another could hear out of it. We see no distinction between that sort of action and permitting an outsider to use an extension telephone for the same purpose.

It is remarkable that the inference drawn by the Court should have appeared before it with such clarity. Affirmative propositions are not always derived logically from negative expressions. The interception contemplated by Congress cannot be likened to the interception that occurs in a football or basketball game, where the ball is prevented from reaching the hands of the intended receiver. Communications by telephone reach the receiver and intercepter simultaneously. Following the logic of the Court, a potential receiver could have his own line tapped so that another might listen in without using an extension telephone. So far as the sender is concerned, there is as much of an interception whether his own line or that of the receiver is tapped. What then would be the meaning of the words "no person not being authorized by the sender?"

Instead of drawing affirmative inferences from negative expressions, the Court should have examined the meaning of "no person not being entitled thereto." What receivers of telephone conversations do is not determinative of the question as to who is entitled to receive a particular communication. The answer lies in the intention of the sender. The Court pointed out that violation of section 605 involved punishment up to a fine of $10,000 and a year in jail, and certainly every secretary directed to hear and record a business communication was not meant to be subjected to the risk of such a penalty. Surely office procedure is not beyond the contemplation of one engaged in a business communication, just as a group conversation between relatives or friends over the telephone is commonplace. Can these be logically compared to the eavesdropping of police officers invited by the receiver?

Associate Justice Frankfurter wrote a dissenting opinion, in which he was joined by Associate Justice Douglas. He stuck to the plain meaning of the words "no person not being authorized by the sender." These words meant what they said. As for secretaries, he looked upon them as the "alter egos" of their employer:

> And so, a secretary is fairly to be deemed as much of an automatic instrument in the context of our problem as a tape-recorder. Surely a police officer called in to facilitate the detection of crime is not such an *alter ego*.

As Justice Frankfurter viewed the matter, the police officers in this case occupied the same position as did the officers in the *Olmstead* case, when the Court sanctioned their practice, and in the *Nardone* case, where the Court rigorously enforced the prohibition by Congress of what was theretofore considered a lawful practice.

The height of privacy achieved in the *Benanti* case was not maintained in the *Rathbun* case. Another case, to which the Supreme Court had earlier refused the privilege of review, also fell short of its mark. That case was *Lanza v. New York State Joint Legislative Committee on Government Operations.*

The facts of the case were assumed on the basis of the allegations made in the complaint. Joseph Lanza and his attorney, Sylvester Cosentino, had conversations in the counsel room of the Westchester County Jail on February 5 and 6, 1957. Lanza had been arrested on a charge of parole violation. Unknown to them, officials of Westchester County had surreptitiously installed a tape-recording device, and a reproduction of their conversations was thereby obtained. On April 26, 1957, the newspapers announced that hearings pursuant to an investigation concerning the facts and circumstances surrounding the parole violation would begin on the 29th, and that the "watchdog" committee of the legislature would make public a recording of the Lanza-Cosentino conversations. The parolee and his attorney brought action to enjoin the publication. A temporary injunction was granted, but this order was reversed by the Appellate Division, which also dismissed the complaint. The case then went to the Court of Appeals, and the decision of the Appellate Division was affirmed by a four-to-three vote.

The plaintiffs contended that the publication of their conversations would violate the privilege accorded to the attorney-client relationship by the Civil Practice Act, and such exposure would impair the client's constitutional right to counsel.

Judge Froessel, who spoke for the majority, indicated that the plaintiffs had misconceived the privilege upon which they relied. The pertinent provisions of the Civil Practice Act, he said, merely sealed the lips of the attorney, so that he could not, as a witness, divulge the contents of conversations had with his clients. "The statute does not," he continued, "inhibit disclosures by other persons who have overheard the conversation . . ."

As for the impairment of Lanza's right to counsel, Judge Froessel observed that the interference complained of would be of consequence only if it were connected with a proceeding against Lanza, and that the investigation of the legislative committee involved no such proceeding. The court was in sympathy with Lanza's claim of interference, but declared that matter to be beside the point:

> Of course, we are with the courts below that the secret recording of the conversations in the manner alleged in the complaint was an unreasonable interference with Lanza's right to confer privately with counsel. . . . . However, that is not the issue here; it is the "use" of the recording that is sought to be enjoined. The interference by undisclosed persons has already taken place. It is clear that if such interference had occurred in connection with a proceeding directed against Lanza, any results in determination would be annulled by the courts on the ground that the interference with his right to counsel destroyed his constitutional right to a fair trial. . . .

And so, conceding that a wrong had been done, the majority of the court found itself powerless either to provide redress or to prevent the possible consequences:

The dissenters did not speak in terms of technicalities. They based their views on matters of principles. Their words should be carefully absorbed as we note portions of their respective opinions.

Judge Desmond said:

> We must keep in mind that at this point in this court plaintiffs, alleging that they are about to be injured irreparably and that they have no protection except an injunction, are asking us for no more than a trial. To accept as true their pleading of what is admittedly a gross wrong and then to turn them away without even a trial is confession by this court of futility and impotence.

> .   .   .   .

> Scrupulously we eschew interference with the functioning of the Legislature. This court will not enjoin legislative action as such regardless of judicial views as to its legality. But the protection of a citizen's constitutional rights is a court function and no public official or body is beyond the reach of that judicial power. . . . If the President of the United States can be stayed by the courts from seizing the steel mills during a national emergency, a New York legislative committee can be enjoined from a gross violation of a citizen's personal rights, no less valuable, certainly, than Youngstown's property.

> .   .   .   .

> There is another compelling reason for asserting judicial power here. Our traditional system of trial and appeal in criminal cases simply cannot be operated unless lawyer-client interviews in jails and prisons have absolute privacy . . . .

Judge Dye said:

> I submit that just as the courts are bound, so too are the Legislative and Executive branches of the Government—the safeguards provided by law may not be flouted by either. It is a clumsy subterfuge to say that because the inquiry is not judicial in nature, the Legislature is not bound to observe fundamentals in the discharge of its legislative function. Nothing could be further from the mark. When the citizen's rights are disregarded our cherished freedoms will end and the Government will cease to exist "of, for and by the people."

Judge Fuld said:

> It cannot be too strongly emphasized that this is not the simple case of a third person eavesdropping on two people who, in this telephonic and electronic age, might be expected to anticipate interception and recording of their conversations. This is a case where the state, or one of its subdivisions, actually invited an attorney into a room so that he and his

client might carry on their confidential business in private—indeed, there was no other place where the client could confer with counsel—and, despite the invitation and despite the more basic guarantee or privilege and confidentiality granted by statute, recorded what was said and then, some time later, turned the record over to another branch of state Government. It cannot be the law that the state may be a party to such a practice and urge that nothing may be done, when the recording is sought to be introduced into evidence, to prevent disclosure and publication of its contents.

On October 21, 1957, the Supreme Court of the United States denied a petition asking for a review of the case.

Attempts have been made to alert the community, the nation, and the world as to the destructive power of atomic bombs, hydrogen bombs, and intercontinental ballistics missiles. The power residing in these weapons may be unleashed for destruction or for peaceful uses. If the battle for peace succeeds, and we all survive, what sort of life shall we live? Will scientific advances still be allowed to continue whittling away the meager remnants of privacy? Shall we, as envisioned by writers of science fiction, live in a world where every action and every word is seen and heard through a contraption constructed in a central office? If complacency continues to pervade our thinking, the day will surely come when thoughts of liberty, individuality, and privacy will gradually fade from memory.